MAX'S SANDWICH BOOK

MAX'S SANDWICH BOOK

THE ULTIMATE GUIDE TO CREATING PERFECTION BETWEEN TWO SLICES OF BREAD

MAX HALLEY
BEN BENTON

Published by 535
An imprint of Blink Publishing
2.25 The Plaza,
535 Kings Road,
Chelsea Harbour,
London, SW10 0SZ

www.blinkpublishing.co.uk

facebook.com/blinkpublishing
twitter.com/blinkpublishing

Hardback – 978-1-911600-83-1
eBook – 978-1-911600-84-8

A CIP catalogue of this book is available from the British Library.

Design and illustration by Agostino Carrea
Photography by Howard Shooter
Photograph on p.298 by Tom Turley
Food styling by Max Halley & Ben Benton
Max's Sandwich Shop Logo and Lettering by William Head
Printed and bound by Balto, Lithuania

3 5 7 9 10 8 6 4 2

Blink Publishing is an imprint of the Bonnier Publishing Group

www.bonnierpublishing.co.uk

FOR AGNES

PART ONE
SANDWICHES

31 OF THE BEST SANDWICHES YOU COULD EVER EAT IN YOUR LIFE (INCLUDING SOME CLASSICS FROM MY SHOP)

PART TWO
RECIPES

ALL THE RECIPES YOU COULD EVER NEED FOR MAKING YOUR
OWN INGENIOUS CREATIONS AT HOME

PART ONE
SANDWICHES

PART TWO
RECIPES

MAX'S SANDWICH SHOP.
A LATE NIGHT, HOT SANDWICH SHOP
YOU CAN GET PISSED IN.

"There is always one moment in childhood when the door opens and lets the future in."
Graham Greene

But I'm not going to talk about that – this book isn't about me and making linguine with my bloody grandmother, it's about sandwiches and how brilliant they are.

Fifteen years in the food industry has taught me that the tastiest dishes tend to be so enjoyable because of these six words:

HOT COLD SWEET SOUR CRUNCHY SOFT

Drop the mic, stick a fork in me or whatever, them's the rules, I'm DONE! At The Sandwich Shop, we stick to them rigorously – it's our sandwich mantra. If all six of those things are present in your sandwich, or on any plate of food, you've a horse worth backing. IT'S THE SECRET OF DELICIOUS.

Despite my fat mouth, I'm not a complete plonker. I don't expect anyone to bake the bread they eat at home or to casually whip up mayonnaise for sarnies to be eaten on the train.

We bake our own bread; you can buy it. We make our own piccalilli; the supermarket sells it. We cook beef for 12 hours; you can use leftover stew. Substitutes are there and ready for you. The thick, serious crunch of one of our cassava chips perhaps, could easily be replaced by a Flame Grilled Steak McCoys.

If you do fancy baking, pickling, stirring, shredding, deep frying and all the rest, down tools and head to the Recipes section where there is a recipe for everything we've ever made in The Sandwich Shop and many more things.

Hopefully this book will help gravy be mixed into mayo with carefree abandon throughout the land, stuff crisps into sandwiches from Aberdeen to Lizard Point and make the bastard shops who sell us so many, try a little harder to marry the ultimate convenience food with utter deliciousness.

Go on, say it with me:

HOT COLD SWEET SOUR CRUNCHY SOFT

Now, turn the page, read about the good stuff, get a pot of mayonnaise out, start COVERING some bread in it and for god's sake, pour yourself a drink.

Cheers!   *Max Halley*

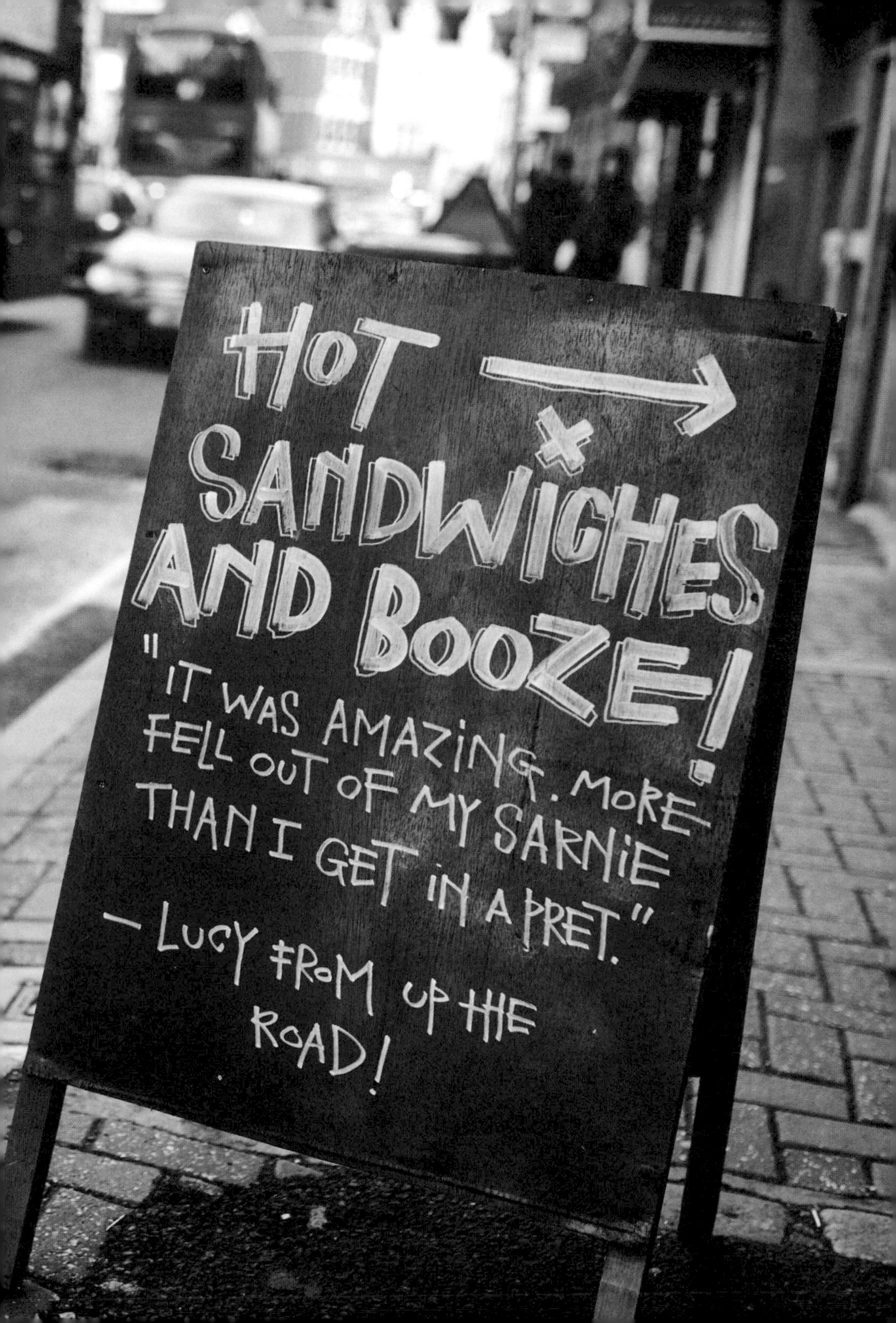
HOT SANDWICHES AND BOOZE!
"IT WAS AMAZING. MORE FELL OUT OF MY SARNIE THAN I GET IN A PRET."
— LUCY FROM UP THE ROAD!

FOREWORD BY NED HALLEY

I was hoping he would be an actor. The Halley dynasty, allegedly descended from the 17th Century astronomer, could do with a less-distant star. The boy Max looked a likely prospect. Extrovert from infancy, he excelled on stage at school, and had a larky time at university in London. His degree was history rather than drama, but he emerged a fully-fledged show-off just the same.

He also acquired an avid interest in food. Millennial London was already turning into today's gastronomic capital and Max was a dedicated carouser. He had discovered his spookily adept sense of taste as well as his appetite. His path was clear. He found casual work in delis and restaurants, did some courses, got a job at the Spanish-food importer Brindisa. He made friends in the business. He has a particular gift for friendship.

Max worked in some serious restaurants including Michelin-starred Arbutus in Soho and Salt Yard branches before managing a new start-up, LeCoq in Highbury. He did some radio broadcasting and began to write lively articles about the restaurant scene for *The Guardian*, *Vice* and others.

His mother, Sheila, and I, were agog. We went to the restaurants, we read his stuff. We knew he was enjoying himself, but we knew too, that he was bolshy. He needed something of his own. "I just want to open a sandwich shop," he would say, when we enquired after his long-term plan.

We had no idea what he intended. But he did. In 2014, Max's Sandwich Shop opened. We helped where we could, and witnessed the creation of an extraordinary enterprise. We are enormously proud of the boy Max.

INTRODUCTION BY AMOL RAJAN

Many a social history of England has tried and failed to identify the origin of the sandwich. Whole doctorates and careers have attended to the task. In fact it is precisely because the origins of this dish are so uncertain - and, by the way, who can really ever say when a particular dish was invented? – that with every passing generation there is some new theory about what makes the perfect specimen. How crisp should the bread be? Rocket or lettuce? Hot or cold?

The thing about all these theories is that they complicate the picture. For me, the ultimate sandwich couldn't be simpler. It's what I eat in Max's, every time.

In the past few years the sandwich has undergone a kind of identity crisis. Brilliant essays and books have been written about how the sandwich both reflects and shapes our culture.

Apparently, by emancipating us from the tyranny of the dining table and cutlery, and by allowing us to eat on the go, the sandwich speaks for a time-poor, cash rich society.

At the same time, and throughout my time as a restaurant critic, food culture was going nuts. New restaurants were opening up every five seconds; TV schedules were filled to bursting with foodie formats; and celebrity chefs were reinventing school meals and food packaging and everything in between. And all this noise, all this complexity, was capable of taking the joy away from food.

I want food to be fun. It was literally this feeling, of wanting to enjoy grub in its simplest forms, that prompted me one afternoon when walking past Max's, to step in. And it is the best gastronomic decision I made in years.

Everything that is glorious and nourishing and vital about food is on offer at Max's place. All the fuss and fidgeting and endless choice and pressure of so much of our food culture gives way to the perfect meal. I don't know about you but when I head out for some grub my checklist goes like this: fantastic food, friendly setting, prompt and thoughtful service, delicious drink, great quiet music in the background and value for money.

Nowhere I know ticks all of those boxes like Max's. While the sandwich has had an identity crisis, his place knows itself. It is endearingly simple and welcoming.

Throughout my time in restaurant criticism, I have seen momentum and fame seep toward the shiny, expensive, and pompous nonsense of high-end restaurants. If you've been lucky enough to eat in and review hundreds of restaurants, you end up pining for that local spot that, like a reliable friend, delivers without fail. Max's does that for me. My only worry is that once word gets out about this book, I'll have to fight you for a table.

THE SANDWICH SHOP BY ED CUMMING

"Where shall we go?"
"Well, there's this place I love called Max's?"
"Sounds great. What does it do?"
"Sandwiches."
"Sandwiches?"
"Yeah."
"Like, stuff in bread?"
"It's a little more complicated than that."

Except, it is and it isn't. This little wood-panelled room at the top of Stroud Green Road might look like the bridge of an old ship, or an Alp-top chalet diner, but in its reinvention of the most staple of staples, the Great British sandwich, it has a revolutionary spirit.

Almost always the man is there himself, doling out London's warmest welcomes, guiding newcomers through his vision. Almost always he will be dressed in shorts and a polo shirt, which give him the aspect of a piratical surfer. But in his bloody-minded quest for perfection, Max is closer to one of those Japanese ceramicists who spend 60 years spinning plain white bowls.

The sandwich's creation myth holds that it is a way to contain a whole meal, the world in your hand. In theory it's one of the great British inventions, like liberalism or the steam engine. But too often this seems like a cruel joke, when we consider the flavourless little triangles lined up in their thousands on refrigerated shelves up and down the high street.

Not at Max's. When Max plonks a brown paper package down in front of you, with a cup of tea or a beer or a cocktail, you know what's coming. Whatever flavours you've gone for, they'll be perfectly balanced, with crunch and tang and warmth and sauce overflowing into strong, fresh bread.

Whatever the situation, Max has the answer. I take my girlfriend there when I'm feeling romantic. I go with my Dad and brothers before Arsenal games. I go after a constitutional up the Parkland Walk, the overgrown disused railway that is London's rugged green answer to the High Line in New York. On a night out in Stroud Green with the lads, I abscond from the pub for 15 minutes to take fuel on board.

Max's secret is that he's governed not by rules but philosophy. Rather than a list of quantities and ingredients, Max's invites you to think to yourself: these are the qualities my sandwich needs. I'll never tire of seeing the greedy delight on the face of a first-timer when they discover that yes, those are shoestring fries in their sandwich. Here's to the host with the most. Mine's a Ham, Egg 'n' Chips.

PART ONE
SANDWICHES

SANDWICHES Nº 01 – Nº 10

MAX'S ORIGINAL

SHOP SANDWICHES

ANYTHING CAN GO IN A SANDWICH

You come out the tube station, head up Stroud Green Road past the Nando's and you're thinking "it can't be *this* far." Over the second set of crossroads and hope diminishes further. Then, can it be? Is that it? The sign slowly emerges like a gorilla from the mist: "HOT SANDWICHES AND BOOZE".

If you're lucky it's raining, so our hand-me-down *Spice Zone* awning will be out, billowing in the breeze, doing its brand-building work.

You head inside and an incredibly handsome, overweight man in a black polo shirt starts waving like an idiot and asking if you're "getting a takeaway or sitting down?" You wonder what the hell is going on, take a seat and are brought ginger water and some menus.

You order, the drinks arrive and you realise how nice the music is. Feeling relaxed you smell the bread baking and start noticing all the cool little things in the room.

When I put the sandwiches down in front of people, they often rub their hands together. It happens all the time; it's the most wonderful thing. They actually rub their hands together.

Arriving wrapped in brown greaseproof paper and sealed with a rubber band, the sandwiches are warm to the touch in a most comforting manner. Opening them is like unwrapping a present. Little pleasant splashes such as these are what makes the place such fun. When you go to the loo, you're in The Cistern Chapel, looking up at a ceiling covered in pictures from a charity shop book. There's a particularly good letter of Hunter S. Thompson's framed above the brick 'n' matches and lots of other funny, silly things.

Whether you're back late, raiding the fridge on a Friday night or making things for the kids' lunchboxes, I very much hope that the sandwich mantra and all our nifty tricks, will leave you with something genuinely useful. The sarnies from The Sandwich Shop that follow, will be a lot of work to replicate at home, but the ideas behind them can be applied to even the simplest things you might make yourself.

Three years ago a journalist asked me why I'd opened the restaurant. I told her "I wanted people to be able to do my three favourite things: staying up late eating sandwiches, getting pissed and not getting ripped off."

It is said that only the humans and the dolphins have sex for pleasure, rather than for purely procreative purposes. That only they have taken a boring biological function and requisitioned it for fun. But a good restaurant does exactly the same – it takes the mere boring biological function of consuming food for energy, and turns it into a joy.

Welcome To Max's
Here's The Options:

1. Ham, Egg 'n' Chips:
Slow cooled ham hock, a fried egg, shoestring fries, piccalilli, malt vinegar and mustard mayo.

2. The Spaniard:
Sweet onion croquetas, sweet herbs, lime pickled onions, baby gem, Morounos mayo.

3. What's Your Beef All About:
Braised Beef Brisket, kimchi, deep fried broccolli and yes, gravy mayo.

4. Pudding:
Choux pastry, black sesame ice cream, caramel and black sesame seeds.

Max's San
For Eating I
DEEP FRIED JACAPEÑO

1. Ham, Egg 'n' Ch
Slow cooked ham hock
piccalilli, malt vinega

2. The Spaniard
Massive onion cro
onions, sweet he

3. This Is What
Barbecoa beef, ta
coriander salad,
sour cream, na

4. Chris' In
Confit guinea
sweet potato

Spuds: A plato
yoghurt, suma

Pudding: A
cherry ice cre

SHOP

TAKING AWAY

...SE BALLS £1 each

£8.50

...g, shoestring fries,

£8.50

...gem lettuce, lime pickled
...os mayo

BEEF IS ALL ABOUT: £...
...narred corn salsa, onion and
...oasted garlic and gravy
cassava chips

ROBOCOQ:
...chen liver parfait, chic...
...till pickle and parsley s...

...HER TINGS:
...ed, fried potatoes, ros...
...n, spring onion
...sandwich with ricotta and s...
...el and tamarind molasses

MAX'S SANDWICH SHOP

MAX'S SANDWICH SHOP

FOR EATING IN OR TAKING AWAY

James' Amazing KimKong Kimchi & Kraut £2.50
Deep Fried Jalapeno Mac 'n' Cheese Balls £1.25 each

1. HAM, EGG 'N' CHIPS:
Slow cooked ham hock, a fried egg, piccalilli, shoestring fries,
malt vinegar mayo
£8.95

2. THIS IS HOW WE SPRING ROLL:
Dre's Pickled Spring Rolls, fresh ginger, coriander, parsley and mint,
KimKong Kimchi, black and white sesame, black bean and MSG mayo
£8.95

3. THE KOREAN GANGSTER:
Soy braised beef, KimKong Kimchi and Kraut, baby gem, parsley,
deep fried noodles, incredibly slutty gravy and doenjang mayo
£8.95

4. ET TU BRUTE? MURDERING THE CAESAR:
Roasted guinea fowl, pickled grape and tarragon salsa, baby gem,
chicory, garlic croutons, anchovy mayo
£8.95

OTHER TINGS:
SPUDS: A plate of crushed fried potatoes, curry powder and garam masala salt,
lime pickle mayo, Bombay Mix, spring onion, coriander and mint
£4.50

TOM'S AMAZING WINGS: Soy and vinegar marinated chicken wings fried
in Surash with guindilla yoghurt and lime pickled onions
£5

PUDDING: Malt loaf crisps, chocolate and hazelnut ice cream, hazelnut
butter, pomegranate molasses, vanilla salted caramel
£6

Please tell us if you've got any allergies. Cheers

Nº 01

HAM, EGG 'N' CHIPS

FILLINGS

Max's Original & Best Focaccia p.114

Slow-Cooked Ham Hocks **p.156**

Piccalilli p.230

1 Fried egg

Shoestring Fries p.214

Malt Vinegar Mayo p.125

"IF WE CAN PUT A MAN ON THE MOON, I CAN PUT HAM, EGG 'N' CHIPS IN A SANDWICH."

When the sandwich arrives, you open the parcel and the smell of spices and vinegar from the piccalilli hits you first, fried egg and ham hock hot on its heels. You begin to get excited and reach for your first half, turning it upward, you see it, the face that launched a thousand chips.

Shoestring fries tumble from the mothership and you scoop them up in your fingers. Crunch. There's egg yolk on your chin and a lick of, what is it, mayonnaise, on your cheek. "THEY'VE ONLY GONE AND MADE MALT VINEGAR MAYONNAISE AND IT HOLDS ALL THEM CHIPS IN PLACE LIKE AMAZING CLEVER LOVELY TASTY FOOD GLUE!" Sip beer. Continue moment.

THE SPANIARD

FILLINGS

Max's Original & Best Focaccia p.114

Massive Onion Croquetas p.202

Morunos Mayo p.125

Baby gem lettuce

Lime-Pickled Onions p.232

Parsley, mint and dill

Everyone, and especially Spanish people, loves croquetas. Everyone, including Spanish people, loves sandwiches. That's how I came up with this one.

The Spaniard was one of the opening three. A perfect illustration of how easily meat can be replaced by the right delicious veggie thing. In this case deep fried, breadcrumbed, nutmeggy béchamel rammed with sweet, sweet onions.

One night a few years ago, a guy had been in four days in a row and had a Spaniard every time. He overheard me talking to another table and asked if it was the veggie option? I said it was and laughing, he told me he'd "eaten this bloody sandwich four times and never noticed there wasn't meat in it." Living the dream.

Our veggie options are as naughty as their meaty companions. Just because you don't think killing animals or breeding them for milk is cool, doesn't mean you want a fucking salad sandwich.

THE ORIGINAL GANGSTER

FILLINGS

Max's Original & Best
Focaccia p.114

Braised Beef For All
Seasons **p.157**

Sauerkraut (p.234 or from
a jar, Krakus is good)

Caraway seeds
(sprinkled on the sauerkraut
in the sandwich)

Parsley

Very Lightly Pickled Onions
p.233

Cassava Chips p.226

Gravy Mayo p.125

"WHAT'S YOUR BEEF ALL ABOUT?"

There is always a beef sandwich on the menu. This one
used to be called What's Your Beef All About? but it went
away for two years and came back, so now it's called
The Original Gangster.

The meat is a rich, brooding stew, cooked overnight
and it has a few excellent bedfellows:

– The punchy bite of onion. Raw, pickled, crispy, baked,
  whatever, onions onions onions.

– Parsley, most refreshing of all the herbs.

– The delicious sourness of anything fermented. Often
  sauerkraut or kimchi. Fermented food is completely
  normal and not a part of some grim, health fad.
  Coffee and vinegar, chocolate and cheese, beer and
  bread, are all products of fermentation.

– Cassava, which we make into crisps. Why not potato?
  Cassava has double the starch content so it goes SUPER
  crunchy and it has a much richer, sweeter, bassier flavour.

– Gravy Mayo – the day before The Sandwich Shop opened,
  we'd cooked beef for the big day and were GUTTED there
  wasn't a way to get the beautiful cooking liquid into the
  sandwich. A *Friends* Moist Maker? It didn't work somehow.
  THEN I HAD IT! We reduced the cooking liquid to beefy
  goo, slammed it in the mayo and we've done it every day
  since. Anyone new in the kitchen is always told "keep
  putting it in until it looks like chocolate sauce."

Nº 04
ET TU BRUTE?
MURDERING THE CAESAR

FILLINGS

Max's Original & Best Focaccia p.114

Perfectly Roasted Fowl **p.176**

Garlic Croutons p.225

Dill Pickle & Tarragon Salsa p.135

Pickled Grapes p.241

Chicory, Baby Gem Lettuce & Parsley

Anchovy Mayo p.125

I love a Caesar salad and all its (seemingly) seventies vibes. That's why I did the grapes. There's nothing seventies about a grape, but there kind of is too. Who knows? Who cares?

We have a lot of spare bread at The Sandwich Shop, so business genius that I am, I had the brilliant idea of putting bread in a sandwich.

"Don't be stupid" the naysayers chorused, "You can't put bread in a sandwich."

Well, it turns out you can, especially if you deep fry it. Haha. The garlic on the croutons is not fresh, it's those granules you get in the supermarket. I'm with the Americans in loving these. Stuff can be SUPER garlicky, but in a really easy, sweet, mellow way.

THE BHAJI SMUGGLER

FILLINGS

Max's Original & Best
Focaccia p.114

Carrot Bhajis p.223

Meera's Coriander, Green
Chilli & Peanut Chutney
p.136

Full fat yoghurt

Lime-Pickled Onions p.232

Spinach

Parsley, mint and coriander

Bombay Mix (London Mix
or Cornflake Mix [the finer
ones] are my two favourites
– Bombay can be a bit
chunky for a sarnie)

Bombay Mix in a sandwich? HHHhahahahahahahhahah.

The famous chef of a very jazzy restaurant was having
dinner in The Sandwich Shop one night and called me over
for a little chat: "This Bombay Mix" he said, "is so SO good.
We make it at work but we've never got it this good."
We buy it in Tesco.

It's such fun using industrially made foods, familiar to
us all, in ways people wouldn't expect. Like the Soreen
Malt Loaf and Jamaican Ginger Cake often used in our
puddings.

Bright, colourful and delicious, this sandwich is a personal
favourite. It's relatively healthy I suppose, but it's no
goodie-two-shoes. As always, it's still got something
deep fried in it!

Andreas "The Dog" Stylianou had the idea for this one and
we turned to my friend Meera Sodha, for inspiration.

She says she's "been going through a slightly obsessive
coriander phase of late. The leaves work well in salads
and give curries a fresh kick but nothing surpasses the
wonder that is this coriander chutney. I always have a jar
of it at home in the fridge. It is best eaten with samosas,
dhoklas or, if you're me, by itself."

When I first made it, I had it with steak, and now we
mix it into the yoghurt for this sarnie.

THE KOREAN GANGSTER

FILLINGS

Max's Original & Best
Focaccia p.114

Braised Beef For All
Seasons **p.157**

Kimchi (p.235 or bought)

Deep Fried Ramen Noodles
p.224

Deep Fried Sweet Potato
Starch Noodles p.224

Baby gem lettuce

Gravy Mayo p.125
(with some doenjang)

I will always love this sarnie. It's from episode one of my *Vice* show, *The Sandwich Show*, where I travel about the place meeting people, pissing about and coming up with amazing, wonderful sandwiches.

A MASSIVE thank you to Alana McVerry and Nicole Cho for all they showed me over those few days and for introducing me to the joys of Korean Barbecue. All this led to one of the great moments of my life: discovering by chance what happens when you throw uncooked sweet potato starch noodles into a deep fat fryer!

THIS IS HOW WE SPRING ROLL

FILLINGS

Max's Original & Best
Focaccia p.114

Pickled Veg Spring Rolls
p.206

Fermented Black Soya
Bean, Honey, Doenjang
& MSG Mayo p.126

Parsley, mint and coriander

A tiny piece of ginger,
peeled and grated

Black and white sesame
seeds (50:50)

Kimchi (p.235 or bought,
we use Kim Kong Kimchi)

Sauerkraut (p.234 or
bought, Krakus is good)

Oh my god! These are the black beans you get in Beef &
Black Bean Sauce and they are AMAZING. They smell like
dark chocolate and taste even richer. So deep in flavour that
blended up, combined with doenjang (Korean miso), MSG
and honey and mixed into mayo, they become something
rich and deeply meat-like. And yet completely veggie.

I thought making spring rolls might be a ball ache, but
actually it's really easy. I watched a few videos online
and two minutes later was playing in the pros. Spring rolls
are such a lovely way of getting crunch, and the pickles,
into the sandwich. They also make something inherently
healthy, into something quite naughty.

TOM OLDROYD'S CURRIED LAMB

FILLINGS

Max's Original & Best
Focaccia p.114

Curried Lamb **p.164**

Deep Fried Cauliflower
p.250

Raita p.142

Pickled Apricots p.241

Red onion

Coriander

This was the first guest sandwich we ever had. There have been others since, but this has remained a favourite! Tom and his Mrs, Meryl Fernandes, are some of The Sandwich Shop's oldest friends, often found on Table 3, smashing mac 'n' cheese balls and sinking Hanky Pankies.

THE BJ BENTON

FILLINGS

Max's Original & Best
Focaccia p.114

Labneh p.138

Sumac-Pickled Peppers
p.239

Beetroot Borani p.151

Parsley, mint and dill

Spiced Fritters p.223

What a legend Ben Benton is. This stunner was his second gift to The Sandwich Shop. His first was training Leia, the original Greek in the kitchen the day before the restaurant opened. He showed her how to make our friend Willie's bread and many other things while I got on with the plentiful other bits of opening the restaurant.

When I asked him to come up with a guest sandwich he suggested going veggie because they're the most difficult ones and he loved the *HOT COLD SWEET SOUR CRUNCHY SOFT* theory. This was a massive success from the moment it arrived and has returned regularly. Look at the colours! And just like The Spaniard, and The Spring Roll, no one ever notices it doesn't have meat in it.

His third gift was to help me write the Recipes section of this book you'll get to later. Without you nothing would work. Love you Ben.

CLAUDIA'S GUAC 'N' EGGS

FILLINGS

Max's Original & Best
Focaccia p.114

Claudia's Guacamole p.207

2 fried eggs

Shoestring Fries p.214
(or some crushed up Ready
Salted crisps or plain
tortilla chips from the shop)

The easiest of all The Sandwich Shop sarnies to make at home.

We only serve this at the weekend because it's such a brunchy/breakfast ting. It's also handy because it's very easy to make vegan. Try losing the eggs and adding some pickles and more coriander.

Claudia Reading, one of my closest family friends, is a beautiful Mexicana and taught my Mum and me to make this guacamole when I was little. The recipe has never changed. It's perfect.

This sandwich is a staff favourite because it is easily tinkered with. Recently we had it for our lunch with fried chicken, again with ham hock meat and often with crushed Cool Original Doritos instead of the shoestring fries.

SANDWICHES Nº 11 – Nº 16

BREAKFAST

Nothing starts the day like a sandwich.

№ 11
THE BLT
(A SATURDAY MORNING SANDWICH)

"PERFECTION IS A LOT OF LITTLE THINGS, DONE RIGHT" MARCO PIERRE WHITE

Got to go out, got to get milk for tea. My hangover's biting hard, my mouth feels horrible and I know that only a sandwich, that cuppa and a large quantity of ibuprofen will keep the despair at bay.

Jos and I nailed so much wine after The Sandwich Shop closed last night that the bin (which David had emptied before he went home) was full when we rolled out at 4am. Jos and his dog Whiskey come to The Sandwich Shop about three nights a week. He's one of my oldest friends, lives down the road and is an incredibly loyal supporter. His wife Olivia is a ceramics conservator and the regular fixer of our much beloved, sometimes kidnapped, and alas, often broken, ceramic ducks. We call her The Duck Whisperer.

I scuttle across the road for goodies. This BLT's a brilliant idea. Sandwiches are a brilliant idea. They eat into our cupboards' ill-fated condiment collections and they don't generally require many pans or much shopping. Today though, I need a few bits as I've been burning the candle at both ends and supplies have depleted.

There's already mayonnaise in the cupboard, so bread, bacon, a tomato, lettuce and the ibuprofen are all I require. Luckily, living in Finsbury Park, I've got loads of great shops, one of London's best pub gardens (at The Faltering Fullback) and an amazing wig shop, all at the end of my road.

But never mind that, I'm on a different mission now – a mission to sandwich – and goddamit, nothing's going to get in my way. I hit up the greengrocer first and squeeze his tomatoes. Picking out the biggest, deepest reddest one, I grab an iceberg lettuce and I'm out the door.

At The Sandwich Shop we use baby gem because I love its faint bitterness and beautiful colours, but in a BLT I think you want iceberg. It keeps better in the fridge and it's ridiculously crunchy.

Next stop, the deli, for their posh Denhay bacon (smoked streaky) because it's actually worth it. I'm not buying fucking sourdough though and I wouldn't buy posh mayo either – there's nothing wrong with Hellmann's.

Finally, I'm roaming the supermarket wild and free, hunting those mini ciabattas they all do. They're ideologically pretty close to the focaccia we make at The Sandwich Shop, especially if you sprinkle water on them and bang 'em in the oven to crisp up.

Crust everywhere, that's what you're looking for. Then the filling can be as juicy as it likes with no fear for the structural integrity of the thing. Sliced bread can be shit for sandwiches when used at the wrong time. It nearly always falls apart (we've all been there with that bastard the butter), it can't handle being condimented sufficiently and everything feels a little too much like a cheap packet sandwich.

Back in the flat, my first job, perhaps unexpectedly, is the tomato. Then the tea and the pills. I cut the tomato into four slices the whole way across its body and chuck the top bit away, lay them on a plate, sprinkle with salt, pepper and sugar and leave 'em to it.

I slice the little ciabatta completely in half horizontally.

Lay 6 slices of bacon, like a boss, in a cold frying pan with no fat in it and put the gas on the lowest of the low. Over 10 minutes I gradually increase the heat ending with browned but not crispy bacon (as is my wont) and LOADS of fat left in the pan. All this takes time, but I've got tea, a massive hangover, Astrud Gilberto on the stereo and it's Saturday, so who cares?

Picking the bacon from the pan with my tongs, I give it a shake and dump it on the tomato plate. Then I tip half the (hot) fat from the pan into a little bowl with a big tablespoon of mayo. It looks like a lot of liquid but trust me, it can take it. Ploop ploop, a few drops of malt vinegar and some Tabasco and stir stir stir! I finish up putting both bits of bread into the pan and frying the insides in the remaining goodness.

Now to build: I go HEAVY with the mayo on the top half, making sure every bit of the bread is covered. Lay gently shaken tomato slices on the bottom and pile the bacon on messily; this is a sandwich – nothing needs to be neat. The only thing you should be anal about is the volume, which should be copious, verging on intimidating.

I get my bread knife and cut a 1cm thick slice of iceberg as you might a loaf of bread, all the way across, trim it to size and pop it on top of the bacon. Tipping ALL the juice from the tomato/bacon plate ALL OVER the lettuce, I put the lid on, give it a squish, cut it in half and take a massive bite.

Feeling a little friendlier towards the world, I lie back, sandwich in hand and the darkness begins to lift.

SAUSAGE & EGG

FILLINGS

A mini ciabatta from the supermarket

5/6 chipolatas or 3/4 whoppers (burger-vanned)

Mayonnaise

Your favourite hot sauce or other condiments

2 eggs, 1 if frying

Butter

"IF THERE'S A SAUSAGE ON THE MENU MAX, ORDER IT." NED HALLEY

When rosy-fingered dawn comes up, get your bangers in a pan. Those little ciabattas from the supermarket keep for days. If they go a bit soft in the bag, sprinkle them with water and slam them straight on the shelf of a hot oven for 3 or 4 minutes. It seems weird to wet bread because it goes floury and sticky, but when it gets hot again and stays there for a while, it regains many of its original charms.

I put Tabasco and malt vinegar in the mayo of all my breakfast sandwiches, but that doesn't mean you have to. Maybe you're a mustard and ketchup person? Do anything you like, but mix them with mayo.

Fry the sausages on a low heat for a long time (about fifteen minutes) turning them regularly. If they are large, burger-van them. This means cutting them in half lengthways, halfway through cooking and squishing them hard.

I'm weird, I like 7-minute boiled eggs crushed with a fork in my breakfast sarnies – you might not be weird – fry away.

Mix half the fat from the sausage pan into the mayo along with the condiments. Fry the insides of the bread in the remaining goodness, then butter the bottom and mayo the top. Sausages in, eggs on top of that and mash mash mash. Lid on. Bit of a squish, cut it in half and get busy.

I once made this with two giant crumpets instead of bread and even more sausages.

A FRIED EGG SANDWICH

FILLINGS

Mother's Pride-type bread. Never toasted

Butter

1 or two frozen potato waffles (optional)

1 or 2 fried eggs

1 tbsp mayonnaise

1 tsp Marmite

Salt and pepper

In my freezer there are normally waffles because my flatmate Neil and I love them! But if you haven't got any, no worries, just have the eggs. If you have got some, read the packet and put them in the oven.

Fried eggs, like kippers, love Marmite. God, kippers would be AMAZING in this sandwich. But I haven't got any kippers, so I spread the mayo (mixed with the Marmite) ALL over the top piece of bread, butter the bottom and fry my eggs. I fry my eggs in a really hot pan so that they're nice and crispy on the bottom and the yolk is still runny. And I have lots of salt and pepper on them.

If you are doing the Marmite, salt your egg tenderly, if at all.

№ 14
THE WHOLE FRY UP
IN A SANDWICH SANDWICH

FILLINGS

Mother's Pride-type bread, toasted

4 slices of smoked streaky bacon

Some baked beans

3 slices of black pudding

2 or 3 Hash Browns (bought or p.205)

1 fried egg

5 chipolatas

Mayonnaise (with malt vinegar and Tabasco)

Any condiments you like

"HOW DO YOU LIKE YOUR EGGS IN THE MORNING?" WITH A KISS? NO MATE! IN A SANDWICH.

Make an entire fry up. You know how. Then put it in a sandwich. Saves the calories from the fried bread doesn't it. God I'm good.

This is a total joy and one of the naughtiest things of the year. Perhaps for only once a year... condiment freely and at your will. But mixed into mayonnaise.

Nº 15
A JAM SANDWICH

FILLINGS

Mother's Pride-type bread

Your favourite jam (I like blackcurrant or cherry best of all!)

Mascarpone (Philadelphia would do)

2 Ginger Nut biscuits, crushed up to sprinkle

As you were, but fleshed out with lashings of mascarpone as my Mum did when I was little!!! YOU. WILL. NEVER. LOOK. BACK.

And sprinkle the biscuits all over the jam, etc., before you put the lid on.

N⁰ 16
PBJ/HAIL TO THE KING

FILLINGS

A mini ciabatta from
the supermarket

Peanut butter
(smooth or crunchy)

6 slices of smoked streaky
bacon (as in the BLT on
p.48)

1 tbsp of jalapeños slices,
chopped up into bits

If you love Elvis, replace the jalapeño with sliced banana
and you have his favourite sandwich. I'm sticking with the
chillies. The pickley spicy peppers are just perfect with the
bacon and the peanut butter – they all make the most of
each other.

Peanut butter top and bottom, plonk the bacon in and
cover that with the jalapeños, give it a squish and open a
cheeky beer. If it's really early, have a Campari and orange
juice. It's a great breakfast drink because, as my Dad says,
"people think you're drinking grapefruit juice!" Hahhaha.

SANDWICHES № 17 – № 22

LUNCHTIME

Why are so many al-desko sandwiches such a sombre affair?
Keep Tabasco on your desk and the sun will always be shining.

Or knock up one of these at home occasionally, take it to work
and eat like a player.

Why should the sandwiches in kids' lunchbox be so sad?
My friend Ben Falk's Dad, Lawrence, used to make him chrain .
(KING OF THE CONDIMENTS p.148) and chopped herring
sandwiches to take to school. And players keep playing.

№ 17
TUNA MELT

I'm sorry but I don't eat much cheese and I can't have a fish and cheese recipe in my book. Keep making it just as you already do.

Nº 18
THE CAFFÈ DOGALI SANDWICH

FILLINGS

The thinnest, crunchiest bread you can find, or one of those ciabattas from the supermarket

6–8 slices of mortadella (as thin as possible)

Truffle cream (mayo and truffle oil mixed together, be bold, p.126 Truffle Mayo)

Artichokes in oil (with vinegar sprinkled on them)

Caffè Dogali is my favourite sandwich shop. It's in the middle of nowhere in North East Florence and at lunchtime everyone's in there: well-to-do Gucci clad ladies, bin men, builders from over the road and so on. All eating sandwiches, drinking wine and breaking the bread together.

The place makes me happy. You should get a coffee and a Fernet Branca to whet the appetite, have a cigarette, then order a bottle of wine and four sandwiches between two.

They give you the illusion of control; you choose your bread (always the really thin crusty focaccia type for me), your meat, your veg and your cream. In Florence, many sandwiches involve what are called creams, but they're actually just mayonnaise with stuff in.

This is my favourite sandwich. As Blackadder's Baby Eating Bishop of Bath and Wells said so well: "Animal, mineral or vegetable, I'll do anything to anything" to get my mitts on one of these.

Really, try it. Make one. You can get everything you need in the supermarket or the deli if you've got one nearby.

Truffle cream both bits of bread, but heavier on top.

Mortadella on the bottom, artichokes on top of that.

Lid on, bit of a squish, GO GO GO.

Viale Malta, 5, 50137 Firenze

N.º 19
TUNA MAYONNAISE
SORT OF...

FILLINGS

A mini ciabatta from the supermarket

2½cm thick pork chop (treat yourself from the butcher) or a few small ones

Veg oil

1 tin of tuna

1 lemon

Lashings of mayonnaise

Something fresh and green, like parsley, watercress would be lovely too

Ready Salted crisps

This sounds weird but ask an Italian (or the internet) about vitello tonnato or, in this instance, maiale tonnato. The other day I had bloody roast chicken tonnato!

Cut the outermost layer of skin off the chop and then cut down through the fat almost to the meat five or six times down the length of the chop. Splitting the line of fat like this will stop the chop curling up when you cook it. Fry it in veg oil covered in salt, for 3 minutes a side in a really, really hot, heavy pan. Lay it to rest on a big plate with foil over it for 10 full minutes. You'll be surprised how much juice you get for your mayo.

Drain the tuna, empty the can on the chopping board and CHOP CHOP CHOP through it a load of times. Whack the tuna and the juice of half the lemon in a bowl along with four tbsp of mayo and lastly the resting plate juices, once the time is up. Mix it all up until it's nice and creamy looking. You will need to add more mayo. It'll take loads.

Tuna mayo the top and bottom of the sandwich.

Now the chop's had its time, slice it into big, thick chunks and put them neatly in the sarnie with the greens. Squeeze the other half of the lemon over, perhaps some salt and sprinkle some crushed crisps on the inside of the top bread and prepare to blow your mind.

There'll be loads of mayo left, but there should be. Have the same thing tomorrow.

N.º 20
FISH FINGER

FILLINGS

Mother's Pride-type bread

Butter

6 frozen fish fingers (see
p.196 for a recipe for posh
ones if you fancy it)

Lemon juice

Ketchup and Salad Cream
(mixed together equally)

A pack of Scampi Fries
(crushed in your hand)

Ketchup and Salad Cream is SO good. But I've got
something else for you. We once blended a pork pie
at work until smooth and mixed that into Salad Cream!
We had it like crudités. Dunking sticks of raw veg into it.
And even slices of pork pie!!!

Butter the bottom, put the fish fingers on and squeeze
lemon juice over. Sauce the lid generously and sprinkle
the Scampi Fries everywhere. Lid on. Bit of a squish.
Sit down to a nice re-run of The Bill or something.

Nº 21
PINE NUT TARATOR
AND CABBAGE

FILLINGS

Soft white, sliced bread, toasted. This is amazing with naan-type flat breads too

1 nice firm pointy cabbage (hispi or sweetheart or something)

Olive oil

1 lemon

Pine Nut Tarator p.141

Tarator is incredibly creamy, simple, coincidentally vegan and absolutely delicious.

Ben Benton and I used to run a restaurant called LeCoq together. He was the chef and I was the manager. One of his most delicious starters was this sandwich, without the bread. Grilled hispi cabbage with pine nut tarator. I started making it at home as a little sandwich to kick off barbecues.

Cut the cabbage in half from tip to base. Then cut each half into three the same way. Boil them in a large pan of water until the core begins to soften just a little. At this point tip the water down the sink and run the cold tap over the cabbage bits until they're cold. Then leave them face down on a tea towel to dry out.

Get a frying pan really hot, or a griddle pan if you have one (or the barbecue). Drizzle olive oil on the cabbage segments (now on a plate) and put them in the scorching hot pan or griddle until they are blackened and burned on the outside. Put them on the piece of bread, a heavy covering of tarator, more olive oil and some lemon juice, lid on and eat.

This is a life affirming thing. How can something so simple be so complete and so delicious? WHO KNOWS! Just make it and eat it.

Nº 22
A HAM SANDWICH

FILLINGS

A mini ciabatta from
the supermarket

Cold butter

Plenty of cooked ham

A small handful of
halved cornichons
(they cling better)

Long live the ham sandwich!

Slice the butter thickly and put it on the bottom
of the bread. Cover it with ham, sprinkle the cornichons
all over. Lid on. Get it in ya.

I wouldn't necessarily advise it, but you could butter
the top too.

This is every bit as lovely with slices of salami or a
big smear of yummy fish pâté (p.197).

SANDWICHES № 23 – № 24

TOASTED

Cheese legend Holly Chaves, is addicted to delis and a toasted sandwich master. In possession of one of Britain's best-stocked fridges she is Master Splinter to my Michelangelo.

And just so we are clear, these are Brevilles, not some sourdough, fried in a pan bollocks. It's called a proprietary eponym when that happens!!! Like Hoover.

There are many toastie recipes in the world, sweet ones and savoury ones. These are my favourite two. Do anything you like, after you've taken these two out for a drive.

Nº 23
A PIZZA TOASTIE
FOR WHEN YOU'RE WATCHING THE NINJA TURTLES MOVIE AT 3AM AND ALL THE PIZZA JOINTS ARE SHUT

FILLINGS

Mother's Pride-type bread

Mayonnaise

6 slices of mortadella
(thin as possible)

2 tbsps passata

Half a scamorza
(if you can find it) or a
cheap mozzarella ball,
sliced in rounds after
being drained and left
in the fridge on a plate to
dry out for an hour or so

Dried oregano

There's a chance I put
some 'nduja that was
in the fridge in here too
but I can't remember

The picture shows two toasties, but I'm so greedy I'd try and get this much in one.

Turn on the toastie machine so it starts getting hot.

Mayo the outside of the slices of bread. It browns MUCH better than butter because it's made of oil and egg. Even though you've mayo'ed it, put the bottom slice down on the chopping board. Pile on the mortadella extravagantly. Good splosh of passata, a big sprinkle of oregano and the scamorza or mozzarella plonked on top. Top piece of bread on. Try and close the lid.

If you've put enough in the sandwich, getting the lid closed will be an absolute bastard. I've snapped handles off two of Holly's machines. Now we use a brick.
A clean brick, of course.

Cook until golden and beautiful. Get back in bed and watch Michelangelo kick some ass!

№ 24
HOLLY CHAVES'
PUDDING TOASTIE

FILLINGS

Mother's Pride-type bread

Butter

Mascarpone

A banana

Salted Caramel (p.282, alternatively, buy a pot in the supermarket or mix some salt into Carnation Caramel)

Biscuit spread like that Lotus Biscoff, or p.288, shortbread or digestives is my favourite

Pomegranate molasses if you have any, otherwise, a tiny squeeze of lemon

It may sound stupid, but try this with bananas that have been in the freezer for at least three days. You don't have to of course but it's AMAZING if you do. Once defrosted they'll be black and horribly soft and look all gross and mooshy inside. But, they're unspeakably delicious. This is how you get a banana to taste how we imagine them to be.

AND THAT BISCUIT BUTTER STUFF!!! Have you had it? That Lotus Stuff?? I recently discovered it and biscuit butters have become an obsession. We make them at The Sandwich Shop with shortbread!! Warmed up, it's one of the greatest things ice cream has ever met.

Turn the toastie machine on.

Butter the outside of the slices and turn them over. I know, it's all sticky and weird but it'll be alright! Biscuit spread on both. Two big dollops of mascarpone in the right places so the machine goes over them not through them! Same of Banana moosh and cover the whole lot in salty caramel.

If you've got any pomegranate molasses kicking about, get some of that in too or squeeze a bit of lemon on there.

Put the lid on the sandwich and close the machine.

Wait.

Remember the inside of sandwiches like these are HOTTER THAN THE SUN. Especially when there's sugar involved.

SANDWICHES № 25 – № 31

LEFTOVERS

Do you remember the quote from the beginning of this book? "Anything can go in a sandwich!" Two pieces of bread are a vessel and all can sail in her. All you have to do is look at the contents of your fridge and cupboards a little differently.

Leftover meals are a brilliant place to begin – they have already been complete plates of food, so you can attend immediately to the sandwich at hand.

Say you've got leftover stew, boiled potatoes and those carrots no one really went for. I'd be thinking about vinegar and cumin on the carrots and parsley to join them. Wondering if those spuds could be sliced and fried up all crispy? I'd check if there were any pickles or some kraut hanging about? And I would DEFINITELY ponder the saturation point of stew juice and mayonnaise.

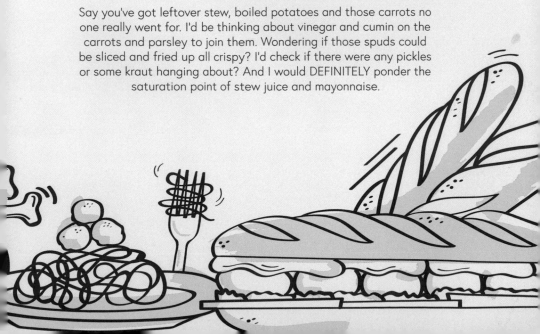

N⁰ 25
SPAGHETTI BOLOGNESE

FILLINGS

Whatever bread you
like, softer the better
for this one

Leftover bolognese sauce

Leftover spaghetti

3 eggs (maybe more,
maybe less, depending
how much pasta there is)

Lettuce-y salad or herbs
of your choosing

1 heaped tbsp
of mayonnaise

Take your leftover spaghetti bolognese, which will be cold
and stuck together. Cut through the cold pasta cake with
a knife into 3 or 4 lumps.

You're aiming for a sort of pasta-omelette-tortilla-frittata
hybrid here. I like it looser, with less egg, some like it firmer,
with more egg.

Beat the eggs in a bowl, throw the spaghetti in along
with the sauce if they were separate. Add anything else
you like, hot sauce, bloody cheese, herbs, grated onion,
fried breadcrumbs, Worcestershire sauce, you know the
score, hands in MOOSH MOOSH MOOSH.

This is always messy. Sometimes it will hold together in
the pan, sometimes it won't. Just leave it be at first for
a good while, so it has the chance to cling together.

Get your smallest (omelette) frying pan really hot, with
some olive oil in it, so the pasta patty can form a crust
and go golden brown with a texture like sun. A little
burning isn't an issue (think of lasagne's crunchy bits).
Oh God! Now I'm thinking about lasagne. What an
amazing sandwich lasagne would make…

To turn the cake over, the sensible thing to do is slide
it out on to a plate, put another plate on top, flip it over
quickly, and slide it back in the pan. Or put it under the
grill. Occasionally I try to flip it like a pancake. Sometimes
it's worked like a dream and sometimes it's been a total
disaster and I've ended up with egg on my fucking face.
At someone else's house? Give it a go. Hahah. Anyway,
dress your lettuce and don't forget about mayo.

Nº 26
BÁNH MÌ

FILLINGS

A mini baguette

Cheap pâté

Leftover Sunday roast meat

Pickles (I had guindillas aka kebab shop chillies and some lime pickled onions)

1 packet of pork scratchings, bashed up

Salad stuff (I had an old carrot I sliced with my veg peeler and half a red chilli)

Fresh herbs (ideally coriander and mint), left in whole leaves

Sriracha Mayo p.124

You can't not love meat and pâté. What a joyful way to use up leftover Sunday roast meat.

This is an absolute joy. Whatever you've had, pork, beef, lamb, chicken or a fucking nut roast, bánh mì it. One trip to the shop and you've got a lovely sprightly end to your weekend and an easy Sunday dinner for everyone.

If you're in the supermarket on Saturday, grab those dinky packs of mint and coriander, a jar of perky looking pickles and a pack of whichever cheap pâté seems most appealing. Perhaps the one that matches your roast? And a bag of Pork Scratchings.

Cut the bread in half lengthways but not all the way through (if you go all the way, it's not the end of the world). Scrape out the soft bread inside and smear a thick layer of pâté on the bottom. Put your leftover meat on top, then the pickles and bashed-up scratchings.

Next comes the veg salad and herbs, mixed together and in abundance. Lastly, the lid, which should be completely covered in the bright red mayo you've made.

This loves a cheeky beer. Put your feet up, close your eyes, can you hear the waves? You're on a beach in Vietnam. Pull a sickie and you can still be there tomorrow. Having another bánh mì for lunch.

A BOXING DAY MONSTER

FILLINGS

A massive piece of focaccia or a mini ciabatta from the supermarket, or something… It might be Boxing Day, so anything will do

150g leftover turkey or whatever you have

2 heaped tbsps mayo

2 tbsps leftover gravy

1 tsp of your favourite condiment (mustard, cranberry, horseradish, etc.)

5–6 leftover raw Brussels sprouts

1–1½ carrots

½ a baby gem lettuce

A big handful of parsley

1 tbsp lemon juice or vinegar, plus extra for the patties

2 tbsps of your best olive oil or posh rapeseed oil or something

A two finger, one thumb pinch of salt and some pepper

Leftover roast potatoes, bread sauce, cooked veg, stuffing etc., the soft stuff

1 egg

1 packet of pork scratchings or Ready Salted crisps or both

Goose fat or butter

I originally wrote this for the Observer Food Magazine:

I feel relaxed and comfortable as the madness of Christmas winds down, and I take great and patient pleasure in the careful construction of one of my food events of the year: the Boxing Day Sandwich. It is an embodiment of the very spirit of Christmas. All the stragglers, the leftovers and the overlooked, brought back together the day after Christmas, to make something truly delicious.

We go to the pub on Boxing Day as early as hangovers allow and I always buy an extra bag of pork scratchings – and some crisps – to take home and slap in my mega sarnie.

The only thing you can get wrong when it comes to this sandwich is not making it big enough. This should be the biggest sandwich of the year. By miles.

Chop up the turkey, put it in a pan, cover it in gravy if you have enough, otherwise a splash of water will do, set it aside.

Stir together the mayo, gravy and your condiment until completely integrated and set aside. If you heat the gravy up a bit it will mix in better.

Ready your veg, which is the sandwich's salad element. I'd use my veg peeler on things like carrots or parsnips and finely slice/shred sprouts or cabbage. Don't be too tough on the lettuce and parsley. Rip it don't cut it. Put it all in a bowl. Take your leftover roasties, bread sauce, cooked veg and stuffing and mash them in a bowl with a fork. Add more pepper, more salt and a nice squeeze of lemon juice. A bit more of your condiment of choice if you so choose. Then crack an egg into it. Mash. Mash. Mash. Use your hands to squeeze everything into 2 patties and get the egg properly incorporated. If you have the time, half an hour in the fridge will help them hold together when you fry them. Make them roughly half the size of your sandwich so the knife can go between them when you cut it in half later. And don't make them too thin. You want soft inside, crunchy outside post-frying.

Run down to the pub to get the pork scratchings or Ready Salted. Give the scratchings a go with a wooden mallet or a rolling pin, still in the bag, to break them into little teeny chunks. If you've got crisps, open the bag and give them a few crushes with your hand. Put your pan of turkey on the cooker over a medium-high heat.

Put your frying pan on with some goose fat or butter in it, again on a medium-high heat. Let the pan get nice and hot and slide your little bubble-esque patties in and turn the heat down to medium. Leave them be until you're worried they're burning a touch then they'll be less likely to fall apart when you flip 'em over. You want a nice tasty, crunchy, golden crust.

»

« Smear your mayo all over the top layer of your bread. Cover every bit.

Mix up the lemon juice (or vinegar), posh oil and salt to make a vinaigrette. Ideally, stick it all in a jam jar or something with a lid, so you can shake it to emulsify, otherwise your whisk is your friend.

Shake your jar of vinaigrette like a mad person. Tip the contents over your raw veg salad and toss it all about.

Cover the bottom piece of bread in the hot turkey. Not too much gravy/liquid though or the bread might begin to break up. And keep the remaining gravy.

Plonk the bubble-esque patties on top of that. Dressed veg/salad on top of that. Sprinkle the crisps and/or scratchings all over the mayo (about half a pack of each per sandwich).

Lid on. Bit of a squish. Cut in half with your biggest, sharpest knife right between the patties. Pour the leftover gravy from the turkey pan into a warm, flat little bowl for dunking the sarnie in.

Pour a large beverage of your choice. This is Boxing Day and all food should be accompanied by some kind of drink. Sit in front of the telly. Close eyes and feel all Christmassy and glad to be alive.

Take another bite.

"OH THE WEATHER OUTSIDE IS FRIGHTFUL,
AND MY BOXING DAY FRIDGE IS DELIGHTFUL,
WE'VE RUN OUT OF CHESTNUTS I KNOW,
BUT I'LL LET IT GO, LET IT GO, LET IT GO.

I'M BASHING THE SCRATCHINGS FROM MY STOCKING,
AND GIVING YESTERDAY'S TURKEY A CHOPPING,
I'M PUTTING CRISPS IN MY SARNIE LIKE A PRO,
GIVE IT A GO, GIVE IT A GO, GIVE IT A GO.

THIS IS MY FAV'RITE SANDWICH OF THE YEAR,
AND THE MIX OF FLAVOURS LOVES A BEER,
WHEN MY LEFTOVER SARNIE GOES DOWN A STORM,
IT MAKES ME FEEL ALL NICE AND COSY AND WARM.

YOU'VE GOT TO BUILD IT UP LAYER BY LAYER,
AND SAY YOURSELF A LI-TTLE PRAYER,
LONG AS YOU MIX SOME GRAVY IN YA MAYO,
YOU'LL HAVE NO NEED OF MISTLETOE, MISTLETOE, MISTLETOE."

ANOTHER EQUALLY EPIC
BOXING DAY MONSTER

FILLINGS

1 large focaccia, cut into
4 equal pieces

8 thick slices of ham

8 thick slices of roast turkey

Pickles:

250ml white wine vinegar

125g caster sugar

1 cucumber, halved
lengthways, and cut
into half moons

2 celery stalks, finely sliced,
on a slant is nice

Chicory and Parsley Salad:

1 tbsp lemon juice

2 tbsps olive oil

2 red or white chicory
heads, shredded

A handful of flat-leaf
parsley leaves

Paxo Croquetas:

½ small onion, finely
chopped

40g butter

50g plain flour

375ml full fat milk

A pinch of ground nutmeg

1 bay leaf

45g Paxo sage & onion
stuffing mix

1 egg, beaten

50g breadcrumbs

Sunflower or vegetable oil,
for frying

Turkey Scratchings:

Leftover roast turkey skin
cut into bite-sized pieces

Pickled Walnut Mayo:

4 pickled walnuts, drained
and finely chopped,
completely mashed up
too is good

8 tbsps mayonnaise

I originally wrote this naughty little number for the Christmas issue 2017 of *Olive* magazine. It makes sandwiches for four VERY hungry people. It wasn't meant to be made with leftovers but to be more of a fantasy Christmas Sandwich.

To make the pickles put the vinegar, sugar and 125ml water into a saucepan. Heat until the sugar dissolves, then cool. Pour the liquid over the veg and leave for at least 2 hours (or preferably overnight). Whip up a little cartouche (p.158) to go over the top of the liquid and keep everything submerged.

To make the croquetas, fry the onion in the butter until very soft (about 20 minutes). Stir in the flour and cook for 3–4 minutes to make a roux, then gradually add the milk. When all the milk is incorporated, add the nutmeg, bay leaf and Paxo mix. Cook for 5 minutes, stirring all the while. Line a baking tray with baking paper. Tip in the croqueta mixture and spread out into a layer approximately 1cm thick. Leave to cool, then chill for at least 2 hours (or preferably overnight) until completely set.

To make the turkey scratchings, put the skin on a non-stick baking tray. Bake at 190°C/fan 170°C until you have really crisp, crunchy skin.

To make the mayo, combine the walnuts and mayo, and season.

Tip the croqueta mixture out onto a board and cut into 4 pieces, each roughly the same size as your chunks of bread. Dip each in flour, then into a bowl of beaten egg, followed by a bowl of breadcrumbs, then shallow-fry in the oil until crisp and golden. Keep warm in a low oven.

To make the salad, either whisk the lemon juice and olive oil with some salt and pepper or put it all in a clean little jam jar and shake it like a bastard. Dress the chicory and parsley.

To assemble the sandwich, cut each piece of focaccia in half horizontally. Spread the mayo over the lids. Chicory salad on the bottom, then some turkey, the croqueta, some ham, a sprinkling of pickles and the scratchings on the mayo. Lid on, bit of a squish, get mash up.

Nº 29

THE MEATBALL SUB
'JUST BALLS, NO SAUCE'

FILLINGS

A mini baguette

A little bag of grated mozzarella and a ball of the stuff too

6-ish leftover meatballs, if they're big, break them up a bit

Leftover tomato sauce (p.143, or passata if you can't be arsed)

Dried oregano

Mustard (I'm partial to French's here, but it's just as great with Dijon)

That's what my sister Lydia used to say when our Mum made spaghetti and meatballs when we were kids.

If you haven't had spaghetti and meatballs and just fancy making this, there's a recipe for the sauce on p.143 and the balls on **p.169**.

Separate the mozzarella ball from its liquid and leave in the fridge on a plate for a few hours to dry out.

Get your oven on at 180°C. Re-heat the meatballs and sauce together in a pan with loads of dried oregano and a splash of water.

Slice the baguette in half down its length but not all the way through. You want it to still have a hinge. Scrape out the soft bread and use it to dunk in the balls to see if they're hot/tasty enough. Tinker accordingly.

Smear mustard thinly all over the bread. You could go mad and mayo too, but just this once, I wouldn't.

Sprinkle grated mozzarella all over the inside of the baguette. You might need a weight (chopping board?) to hold the bread open. Dot slices from the whole mozzarella ball all over the inside too. Put the balls and sauce down the middle of the baguette and close it up. Wrap the whole thing as tight as you can in a generous amount of foil and pop it in the oven until all the cheese has melted. This often takes longer than you might think, probably about 10 minutes. When the outside is too hot to touch, the inside tends to be perfect. You can always put it back in if the cheese hasn't melted properly.

№ 30
LAST NIGHT'S TAKEAWAY

FILLINGS

A mini ciabatta or something crusty

Whatever curry you had

Leftover side like saag aloo, for example

That amazing mint sauce stuff and some lime pickle

That bag of salad you always get (with the lemon squeezed on it)

Crushed up poppadoms

There are no rules with this kind of thing, because I have no idea what leftovers you've got, or even what takeaway you had. For the sake of argument let's say this week's takeaway was from the local Indian restaurant.

If you had a meat curry, chop the bits up smaller and put them and the sauce in a pan, with a splash of water and the saag aloo, or whatever you had. Start heating it up. Put the hot curry & co. on the bottom of the bread, smear the top with the condiments, cover the meat in the salad and crush two whole poppadoms on top of that.

If you wanted, you could mix some of your curry's sauce with the other condiments like a player. And as always, never, ever, be afraid to get the mayonnaise out.

N⁰ 31
AN ICE CREAM SANDWICH

FILLINGS

Mother's Pride-type bread, or anything nice and soft, toasted

Lashings of ice cream, whatever flavour you've got, taken from the pot in slithers with the spoon, not curled into balls

Lotus Biscoff biscuit spread (crunchy one if there's a choice) or p.288

½ tsp Horlicks (or cheap own-brand alternative)

Maybe some leftover nuts, or crushed biscuits if they're lying about

Salt

Pomegranate molasses (blame Ottolenghi)

"LIFE'S A SHIT SANDWICH. AND IT'S ALWAYS LUNCHTIME."

Unless you're putting ice cream in that sandwich, in which case life's a dreamboat.

This little legend is great for using up any manner of sweet things you might have lying about. Instead of the Biscoff stuff you could use peanut butter or jam or Nutella. Caramel in some form would be brilliant. You could make a Snickers!? Honey, mascarpone, yoghurt, custard, they're all there for the taking. Give 'em all a go – this one's got legs!

Get the ice cream out 5–10 minutes in advance. And make the toast too because you want it cold by the time you make the sandwich.

Biscoff spread both bits of toast followed by a generous covering of ice cream. Sprinkle the Horlicks and crushed nuts, etc., all over the ice cream with the faintest sprinkle of salt.

Drizzle pomegranate molasses's miracle mix of sweet and sour over everything and pop the lid on. Slice in half and eat.

ALL THE SANDWICH SHOP'S SANDWICHES

HAM, EGG 'N' CHIPS
Slow cooked ham hock, piccalilli, a fried egg, shoestring fries, malt vinegar mayo

THE SPANIARD
Massive Onion Croquetas, sweet herbs, lime pickled onions, baby gem, Morunos mayo

THE SPANIARD 2
Pea, mint and labneh croquetas, raita, sweet herbs, lime pickled onions, baby gem lettuce

THE BJ BENTON
Spiced fritters, labneh, beetroot borani, sweet herbs, sumac pickled peppers

THE BHAJI SMUGGLER
Carrot bhajis, coriander, green chilli and peanut chutney, yoghurt, sweet herbs, spinach, pickles, actual Bombay Mix

THIS IS HOW WE SPRING ROLL
Dre's pickled veg spring rolls, grated fresh ginger, coriander, parsley and mint, James' Kim Kong Kimchi and kraut, fermented black soya bean, honey, doenjang and MSG mayo, black and white sesame seeds

GUAC 'N' EGGS
Claudia's guacamole, two fried eggs, shoestring fries

WHAT'S YOUR BEEF ALL ABOUT?
Braised Beef, kimchi, deep fried broccoli, and very naughty gravy mayo

WHAT'S YOUR BEEF ALL ABOUT? 2
Braised Beef, sauerkraut, cassava chips, incredibly slutty gravy mayo

WHAT'S YOUR BEEF ALL ABOUT? 3
Braised beef, parsley and pomegranate slaw, charred greens, cassava chips, barbecue hot sauce

WHAT'S NEIL GILL'S BEEF ALL ABOUT?
Braised beef, sauerkraut, caraway, chrain, parsley, baby gem lettuce, cassava chips, crème fraîche, fresh horseradish

THIS IS WHAT ARTHUR'S BEEF IS ALL ABOUT
Barbacoa beef, tomato and charred corn salsa, onion and coriander, roasted garlic, chipotle and gravy sour cream, nachos and cassava chips

THE ORIGINAL GANGSTER
Braised beef, sauerkraut, caraway, very lightly pickled onions, parsley, cassava chips, incredibly slutty gravy mayo

THE KOREAN GANGSTER
Braised beef, James' Kim Kong Kimchi and kraut, two different types of deep fried noodles, parsley and baby gem lettuce, gravy and doenjang mayo

CHRIS' INFAMOUS ROBOCOQ
Confit guinea fowl, chicken liver parfait, chicory, dill pickle and parsley salsa, sweet potato shoestring fries

ET TU BRUTE? MURDERING THE CAESAR
Roasted guinea fowl, pickled grapes and tarragon salsa, baby gem lettuce, chicory and parsley, garlic croutons, anchovy mayo

TOM OLDROYD'S CURRY SANDWICH
Curried Lamb, deep fried cauliflower, raita, pickled apricots, red onion, coriander

TOM OLDROYD'S PORK BELLY AND FENNEL SANDWICH
Roasted pork belly, pork scratchings, pickled fennel and watercress, fennel seed and garlic mayo

KEITH
Slow cooked mutton shank, kipper pâté, beetroot and horseradish, gherkin, caper, red onion and watercress salad, beer dressing, crisps

PART TWO
RECIPES

Ladies and Gentlemen, this is Ben Benton. Ben, this is all the lovely people who bought the book! Ben won't talk about himself, so I'd like to:

Ben is my friend and I love him immensely. We met running a restaurant called LeCoq together. After fifteen years in the food and restaurant game, he is the most naturally talented cook I have ever encountered. My mind is frequently blown by his innate ability to make the simplest things delicious, and the most complicated things simple. He's the first person I would ask to cook me lunch if I could choose anyone to do it. My Francis Mallman.

A little bite of some odd-looking vegetable, a glance at a piece of meat or a smell of a fish's wet bits and somehow, he just knows what to do with it, how it might best be cooked and what will go with it perfectly. This makes him not only incredibly attractive, but an excellent man to sandwich with. Which is why I asked him to do this next bit of the book with me!

In the first half, I have tried to show you how I make sandwiches. What I think about while doing it and as I said before, all my nifty little tricks. Hopefully now, you've had loads of ideas for things of your own to try out! I hope you'll always be mixing things into mayonnaise, and that in the future, some of them might never have been thought of before!

This next section of the book contains not only every recipe for everything we have ever made at The Sandwich Shop, but TONNES of other stuff too! And many of them are Ben's. He's brilliant!! Can you pick his voice out from mine?

You're going to find recipes for mayonnaise, ice cream and all kinds of mad stuff, but don't be put off! You don't have to make anything you don't want – most things can be bought in the shop.

This bit of the book is as much a fantastic list of things to buy and whack in sandwiches as it is a cookbook, for actually cooking from. Which you definitely should do! Give all or any of it a go for God's sake, sandwich the shit out of it.

All these lovely extra things are of course, fantastic in sandwiches, but many are also delicious meals on their own – no bread involved.

Together, Ben and I would like to encourage just generally, the idea of making a delicious dinner for tonight, with a sandwich in mind for tomorrow.

Now, get that massive porchetta you made yesterday out of the fridge and apron up (**p.168**). And get that pot of mayonnaise back out…

BREAD

8 BREADS AND WHAT TO DO WITH THEM

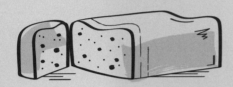

SOREEN MALT LOAF

Butter it so thick you can see your teeth in it, and make yourself a nice cup of tea.

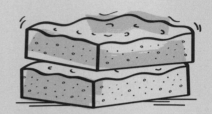

FOCACCIA

The bread we make at The Sandwich Shop. Perfect for everything.

SLICED WHITE/BROWN/GRANARY

Their star shines brightest at breakfast, but they'll be happy anywhere.

BRIOCHE

Good for sweet stuff of course, but surprisingly good for a BLT too.

BAGUETTE

Good for nearly everything – crust everywhere. If filling generously, scrape out the inside.

MINI CIABATTA

The closest bread you can buy in any supermarket to what we make at The Sandwich Shop. Wet it and pop it in a hot oven to crisp up.

ROLLS/ENGLISH MUFFINS

If it's good enough for the Sausage & Egg McMuffin…

SOURDOUGH

Can go fuck itself.

MAX'S ORIGINAL & BEST FOCACCIA

THIS IS THE BEST SANDWICH BREAD THERE IS. AND THE ONLY ONE WE MAKE AT THE SANDWICH SHOP. IT SOAKS UP JUICE WELL, BUT MAINTAINS ITS STRUCTURAL INTEGRITY RIGHT TO THE END. YOU WILL NEVER NEED ANOTHER.

THERE ARE PICTURES ON PAGES 118-119 TO SHOW YOU WHAT STUFF SHOULD LOOK LIKE WHILE YOU'RE MAKING IT.

540g (we use) Shipton Mill Strong White Bread Flour

7g sachet of fast-action dried yeast (Sainsbury's yeast is perfect, it is what we use, and it's amazing)

½ tbsp salt

½ tbsp caster sugar

288ml warm water (ideally 38°C). Read the recipe for a precise, easy way to do this.

50ml extra virgin olive oil (or posh British rapeseed oil, or something similar – let's not be too fussy)

Maldon sea salt

Find an electric mixer with a dough hook, or a large bowl and someone with lots of energy and put all the dry ingredients inside.

Run the cold tap for a bit and put 175ml of cold water in a measuring jug. Boil the kettle and add 113ml of boiling water. This should leave you with water at 38°C. Pour the oil into this. Tip the jug into the mixing bowl (see step 1, p.118–9)

This is much easier on scales than using the jug itself. Put the jug on your scales and remember 1ml of water weighs exactly 1g. God love the metric system.

Mix everything together until you have a dough-like mix, and (out of the bowl) knead it for 6 minutes. If you're using the electric mixer, just start blending for six minutes on the slowest setting. Don't bother mixing before. We've tried longer kneads, and shorter kneads, kneads must and all that, but 6 minutes is perfect (step 2)

If you have a big bowl and a big roasting tray (step 5-6) keep the dough in one lump. If you have smaller bowls and roasting trays, you're going to need to split it.

Pull the dough from the mixing bowl and split it into two halves of equal weight. We do this on scales. Weigh the whole lump, then calculate what the halves should weigh.

It's important to not to be afraid of the dough when you're splitting it. You can pull it about and push it around and it won't mind. Just don't beat it up too much in the process.

Whether you split the dough in two or not you now need to round it a little, neaten it up. Take it in your hands and tuck both the sides, under and in on themselves, so it starts to look like a Super Mario turtle shell (step 3) Do it a

---

few times and turn the dough round. I do it in increments of 90°. It will end up with a smooth-ish top and messier bottom. Sometimes very smooth, sometimes less so. Plonk it in your bowl(s) smooth side up. (step 4)

Cover the bowl(s) with clingfilm or a tea towel and leave somewhere warm (we leave ours on top of the oven) for 1–2 hours until the dough has at least tripled in size. (step 4)

Take a high-sided roasting tray (step 5) and cut a piece of greaseproof paper to cover the bottom and come up the sides. If it's a bit too big like in step 5, it doesn't matter.'

Squirt a bit of oil in the tray, rub it all over the bottom and place the paper on top. It will stick down nicely. You will bake the bread with this paper beneath it to prevent it sticking to the tray. It won't affect the baking of the underneath at all.

Put a glug from your bottle of oil (1 tbsp) into the tray on top of the paper and rub it all around everywhere.

Take the dough out of its bowl and keeping it the same way up, put it in the middle of the tray. Don't be afraid it'll deflate, you're gonna squidge it everywhere now anyway. Push and knead it out all over the tray in as even and level a layer as possible. (Step 5)

I often find it easy to leave too much dough in the middle and not enough in the corners, so watch out for that.

The dough will resist you as you spread it out and bounce back, but be strong and keep pushing to the edges. Tell it where you want it to go with your fingers. As even as possible all over the tray. (Step 5)

If you think you've put too much oil in and it's licking up the sides of the dough when you push it to the corners, don't worry, it likes it.

Once it's mostly spread out, and even if it is still contracting some, which it will, don't worry at all, it's   »

«

gonna rise loads! Sprinkle the surface with plenty of crunchy salt (like Maldon). Be generous, be bold, be a goddamn salt-baller. Cover the tray with clingfilm. Wrap the roll around the tray a few times, don't bother trying to get one little sheet of clingfilm to stick to the tray. Round and round the whole tray. Much easier.

Preheat the oven to 220°C.

Prove for a further 1–2 hours in a warm place, like near the warming oven, until the dough has tripled in size again [Step 6] It will most likely have risen and be touching and sticking to the clingfilm, don't worry, you will be able to (gently) peel it off when it is time to put it in the oven.

Once the dough has risen beautifully, remove the clingfilm and place the tray in the preheated oven for 18 minutes. This gives you the perfect relationship between colour and crunchy crust. If you split the dough in two, bake both loaves at the same time. Even if they're on different shelves it's fine. Leave the bottom one in while you turn the first out of its tray and get it on your cooling rack. [Step 7]

We put the rack on top of the baking tray and with an oven glove covering each hand, carefully turn the whole lot over so the loaf falls on to the rack and doesn't break. Then turn it the right way up again and leave it to cool. Don't leave it on the paper, chuck that out.

Cool for at least 40 minutes on the wire rack. The bread will be soft and lovely, but it needs to cool completely to maintain its structural integrity and lovely fresh fluffiness when you cut it. If you don't let it cool, you will end up with a spongy mess of a sandwich.

Portion the bread when cool and pack with your choice of delicious fillings. [Step 8] If you want to freeze some, portion it up and do so, but don't cut it half like in Step 8. Reheat the bread from frozen, wrapped generously in tin foil, with some oil drizzled on it, in a hot oven until it's soft all the way through again.

1

2

BREAD MAKING

5

6

STEP BY STEP

SAUCES
& CONDIMENTS

PERFECT MAYONNAISE

SANDWICHIEROS (THE FINE MEN AND WOMEN WHO MAKE SANDWICHES PROFESSIONALLY) HAVE KNOWN FOR CENTURIES THAT THE BACKBONE TO ANY FINE SANDWICH IS A RICH, PIQUANT AND FULLY FLAVOURED SAUCE. THIS SAUCE CAN COME IN MANY GUISES, AS THIS CHAPTER WILL BE QUICK TO HIGHLIGHT, BUT THE ONE THAT WE ALL RETURN TO IS MAYONNAISE. THE SANDWICH MOTHER SAUCE.

BELOW YOU WILL FIND A RECIPE FOR THE PERFECT MAYONNAISE. AFTER THAT YOU WILL FIND WAYS TO BASTARDISE, TWEAK, TWIST AND MANIPULATE IT. GO WILD. DO NOT LET OUR IMAGINATIONS CONSTRICT YOURS. GO FORTH AND MAYO.

IT IS IMPORTANT TO POINT OUT HERE THAT WE COMPLETELY UNDERSTAND IF YOU HAVE NO INTENTION OF MAKING MAYONNAISE AT HOME. IT CAN BE A HERCULEAN FEAT TRYING TO EMULSIFY EGG YOLKS AND OIL, SO IF YOU WANT JUST BUY A JAR OF HELLMANN'S.

2 large egg yolks

½ tsp Salt

Juice of ½ lemon (1 tbsp)

1 tsp red wine vinegar

1 tsp Dijon mustard

300ml rapeseed oil
Don't use olive oil,
it's way too strong!

Unless you have forearms the size of ham hocks, find an electric whisk or a food processor. If you do want to whisk by hand, find a very large, clean bowl, a clean balloon whisk and a damp tea towel. Make a doughnut out of the tea towel and sit the bowl in the centre. This will allow you to whisk like crazy and slowly add your oil without having to chase your mixing bowl around the kitchen surface.

Assuming that you've followed the more sensible path and found an electric whisk, place your egg yolks in the bowl, add the salt, mustard, lemon juice and vinegar and whisk together for a full minute until light in colour and slightly aerated. This minor detail is going to make things much easier. The acid, salt and mustard each act on the yolk in their own way and change its molecular structure from "get that greasy oil away from me", to, "look how silky and smooth I'm becoming".

With your oil measured out in a jug start to slowly introduce the oil to the whisked egg yolks in the thinnest stream of oil you can achieve. Whisking all the time, you will notice that the mixture is emulsifying and thickening. Keep going until all the oil is in. If something doesn't look right, read the top of the next page for some mayo saving tips.

Tips to avoid (and if needs be recover from) splitting:

Use your ears. If the sauce starts to slap around the bowl, and oil is staying around the edges, you may be nearing the dreaded splitting. In which case, stop pouring the oil, keep whisking, and keep listening. You will likely have saved it. Now go back to adding the oil. If you are still nervous, you can add a tablespoon of warm water to the sauce and keep whisking – this often brings the mayo back from the brink.

If you do split the mayo, do not fear. Decant the mixture to another container, clean out the bowl and put one egg yolk in it. Whisk it alone for 10ish seconds, and then slowly add the split mixture to this yolk, whisking all the time. Go slowly, and you will bring back the split mayonnaise. Once you have all the split mixture reincorporated, go back to your oil and continue adding it in a slow and steady stream.

TYPES OF MAYO (HOMEMADE OR NOT DOESN'T MATTER)

IF YOU'VE GOT HELLMANN'S, AS I ALWAYS HAVE AT HOME, RATHER THAN HOMEMADE MAYO, JUST ADD ONE BIG TEASPOON OF THE ADDITIONS THAT FOLLOW TO EVERY TWO TABLESPOONS OF MAYO. WE'VE BEEN A LITTLE RESERVED HERE, SO IF YOU'RE MAKING IT AT HOME, FEEL FREE TO ADD MORE OF ANYTHING FOR EXTRA PUNCH!

Sweet herb mayo

Sweet herbs encompass most soft herbs as opposed to the hard herbs like rosemary, thyme and sage. You could draw on any or all of mint, parsley, coriander, dill, oregano, basil and tarragon. If you have leanings to one, two or three of these guys, grab a small bunch of each and blitz them with a splash of oil in your food processor. If you're making mayo, to ensure the flavour is big and rounded in the finished sauce, bang the blitzed herbs into the mayo right at the beginning, when you add the mustard and vinegar.

Lemon mayo

You don't have to be holidaying on the bloody Amalfi coast, wooing a chestnut-skinned local and eating fritto misto de mare to enjoy this mayo. It is amazing with any fried, greasy or fish-related sandwich. Replace the vinegar in the Perfect Mayonnaise recipe with the juice of one entire (unwaxed) lemon. To really pick up the piquant, you could even grate a little zest in the mayo too.

Sriracha mayo

Fire in the fucking hold. The bánh mì bad boy. This guy is hot from chilli and garlic, but has enough sugar and vinegar to have the devil of addiction dancing merrily in your mouth. Replace the lemon juice in the Perfect Mayonnaise recipe with a double measure of sriracha and prepare to become addicted.

Yuzu mayo

Mayo-san, what an honour to welcome you to our sandwich. Yuzu is a Japanese citrus fruit that is somewhere on the spectrum between grapefruit and mandarin. It is pricey, mind, so only lean towards this guy if you're freaking loaded or if someone else is paying. You can find the juice in little bottles on the internet and in some supermarkets. Replace the vinegar and lemon juice in the Perfect Mayonnaise recipe with equal measures of yuzu juice.

The simplest garlic mayo

Aioli we hear you cry. "Sort of", we tentatively reply. Mayonnaise bolstered by the heat of pounded raw garlic cloves is addictive. Call it Arthur for all we care, we're licking it from our fingers anyway. Add two pounded garlic cloves (chopped up tiny, covered in salt and mooshed with a knife or spoon) instead of the mustard in the beginning of the Perfect Mayonnaise recipe and Aioli is your Aunt. If using Hellmann's or something add one clove to every four tbsp of mayo. It gets stronger and stonger as time goes on too.

Garlic & fennel seed mayo

Same ting, different zing. When you are pounding the garlic cloves for Arthur the Aioli, add a tsp of toasted fennel seeds. Bash them up something rotten and add them with the pounded garlic.

Morunos mayo

This old friend is from The Spaniard sandwich on p.28. You're Spanish and love Morunos mayo, what do you add? One teaspoon of sweet smoked paprika, one of cumin powder, one of coriander powder, half a puréed garlic clove, and the juice of half a lemon. When does he add it? Right at the beginning instead of the mustard and vinegar. If you're adding these things to two tablespoons of bought mayo, use a scant half teaspoon of everything.

Gravy mayo

A Sandwich Shop staple. When you are cooking meat, be it a stew or a roast, keep some of the cooking liquid. Sieve it. And reduce it in a pan until it is a tbsp or two of thick, rich, sauce and then add this to a batch of the Perfect Mayonnaise. You can simply beat it in at the end and if it's warm, it mixes in better. Read the Braised Beef For All Seasons recipe on p.157 for further musings on this little legend.

Anchovy mayo

Take 6 anchovy fillets, moosh them up and add them to the Perfect Mayonnaise recipe at the same time as the vinegar and mustard. This is a sandwich sensation with roast lamb, beef and any manner of crisp and fresh vegetable-based fillings. To be honest, it is so addictive, you might just want a small bowlful of it on hand at every meal for dunking and dragging through.

Tuna mayo

If you've never had vitello or maiale tonnato then this might sound a little mystifying. The idea of cold leftover pork or veal covered in a tuna-based mayonnaise sounds, at first, like a culinary travesty. But, it is wizardry of the highest order. Take half a tin of the nicest tuna you can buy, drain it, empty it onto your chopping board and cut through it a load of times. If you're making mayo, dump it in at the same time as your mustard and vinegar. Add an extra half a lemon's worth of juice too. We wouldn't stipulate that you have to use this in a pork-based sandwich, but if you did, it would be all the better for it. Look at the Tuna Mayo, of sorts… sandwich on p.69. If you're adding to 2 tablespoons of bought mayo, add 1 tablespoon of chopped tuna and a big squeeze of lemon.

Malt vinegar mayo

This is one of the great mayonnaises and what we use in the Ham, Egg 'n' Chips sandwich. It is as sharp as a genital put-down and as addictive as poppers. Got a sandwich with rich, fatty hot meat in it? This mayo is your guy. Simply replace the lemon juice and regular vinegar in the Perfect Mayonnaise recipe with malt vinegar. You are welcome.

Kimchi mayo

In Korea the use of kimchi is akin to that of tomato ketchup. But they use it more. The heady fermented heat of this cabbage is outrageous. Add 2 tablespoons chopped up small once you've made your mayo and we will leave to you to fumble for the correct expletive.

»

MORE TYPES OF MAYO (HOMEMADE OR NOT DOESN'T MATTER)

Doenjang mayo

It is those wonderful Koreans again. This fermented soya bean paste is akin to miso. In fact, if that is easier to find, use that instead. Simply add a tablespoon of the doenjang to the base of your Perfect Mayonnaise recipe instead of the mustard and proceed as usual. You might want to hold fire on some of the salt as doenjang (and miso) can be salty little critters.

Pickled walnut mayo

You read us right, we're adding pickled walnuts to a mayo, and we suggest you do exactly the same. Add a couple of blitzed pickled walnuts into the Perfect Mayonnaise recipe along with the mustard and vinegar. If you have a beef-related filling in your sandwich, this mayo will arouse you enormously. Have a look at the picture on p.96. It looks a bit grey which is weird in food BUT WHO CARES IT'S SO FUCKING DELICIOUS!!!

Truffle mayo

Whether you're holding a piece of raw celery, a chip from the chippy, a sarnie you've made or one of Tom Oldroyd's pea and ham croquetas, this is one of the most delicious things you can dunk anything in. Experiment at will and with commitment. Cold roast meats and eggy stuff will all love it. Simply add 2 heaped tablespoons of mayo to 1 level tablespoon of truffle oil and mix, mix, mix. If you've made Perfect Mayonnaise just whisk truffle oil in at the end until it becomes as strong as you like.

Fermented black soya bean, honey, doenjang & MSG mayo

It's them gangster beans again. I get mine in Chinatown. They're sometimes called Preserved Black Beans.

This makes a tiny quantity of bean paste so you might have trouble making it in a blender. Dust off the pestle and mortar if you've got one buried somewhere, or get a big chopping board out. Cut up 10 soya beans as small as you can and grind them until paste-y with the back of a spoon or the side of your knife. Tip a teaspoon of honey on them. Grind grind grind. Add a teaspoon of doenjang and do the same. Sprinkle some MSG in, as much as you'd add salt. Mix this into 2 heaped tablespoons of mayo.

This stuff is bonkers. It tastes like meat, it's incredible. I should probably shoot myself for saying it, but this is the very definition of umami. Madness. If you're making Perfect Mayonnaise, add the paste at the end and whisk it in well. And feel free to add more.

Cooking fat mayo/resting juice mayo

Maybe you've cooked something meaty like bacon and sausages in a frying pan or roasted a chicken or some lamb in the oven. Maybe you've cooked a massive steak that's now on a plate covered in foil, resting into submission. There's fat and/or juice in that pan or on that plate. And you don't want to waste it, so mix it into mayonnaise.

Sometimes, like in the pork chop recipe (see p.69) you might have had the pan so hot the goods left behind are burned. Don't use that stuff – stick with the juices from the resting plate. One flat tablespoon of cooking fat/juice, to 2 heaped tablespoons of mayo.

This doesn't have to be used right away. Just make it and keep it in the fridge for a sandwich with the remains of the day.

Pork pie mayo

We made this at The Sandwich Shop with Salad Cream and it was insane. Now we do it in mayo too.

Put some little pork pies (3–4 from what I remember, or one large one) into a food processor and blend. And keep blending. We're always cooking ham hocks so we splash half a ladle of liquid from the pan into the blender too to help everything get along. You could add a splosh of boiling water from the kettle or some heated up apple juice. The inimitable Claude Bosi used to do this at 2 Michelin starred Hibiscus (with apple juice and fish stock) as a sauce for scallops, and he definitely knows what he's doing.

After about 2 minutes the whole mix begins to warm a little and becomes surprisingly smooth. At this point, mix your pork pie mess into some mayo, season with a touch of salt and vinegar to bring out the flavour of the pie. Eat it with raw vegetables or, rather sinfully, slices of pork pie.

HOT SAUCE

YOU BEST HAVE A MEGA HOT SAUCE IN THE HOUSE. IF YOU DON'T YOU HAVE NO PLACE BUYING THIS BOOK. UNLESS YOU BOUGHT IT TO LEARN HOW TO MAKE HOT SAUCE, IN WHICH CASE, COME ON IN, THE WATER IS HOT AND FRUITY AND TASTES DELICIOUS SPLOSHED ALL OVER EVERYTHING.

ME AND MY FRIEND JUSTIN CLARK, LOVE HOT SAUCE. HE WAS ONE OF THE SANDWICH SHOP'S FIRST CUSTOMERS AND IS A TOTAL BOSS. THIS ONE'S FOR YOU MATE. UNTIL OURS IS READY TO BE RELEASED INTO THE WORLD!

---

1 tsp olive oil

3 Scotch bonnet chilli peppers, finely chopped, seeds and all, stalks removed. If you like it hot, really hot, as some do, you could go with more chillies. Good luck!

240g fresh, ripe pineapple, peeled and chopped into chunks

120g fresh, ripe mango, peeled and chopped into chunks

120ml white wine vinegar

1 tsp caster sugar

1 tsp salt

Place a large, heavy-bottomed saucepan over a high heat and add the olive oil to the pan.

After a few moments, once the oil is hot, add the chopped chillies to the pan and allow them to sizzle for 30 seconds. You don't want to cook them as such, but it's nice when the skins get a little blistered.

Next, add the pineapple and mango to the pan and continue to cook over a high heat for 3 minutes, after which the fruits should be giving way and becoming compote-like. At this point, add the vinegar, sugar and salt, bring to the boil, reduce the heat to low and continue to cook, stirring occasionally, for 10–15 minutes.

Once the sauce has reduced and become one, taste for seasoning, adding a little more vinegar for sharpness, salt for depth of flavour and sugar if it needs a little sweetness. We cannot taste your chillies, pineapple or mango for you and they can all taste different depending on the season, ripeness etc., so you'll need to rely on your own taste buds at this point.

If the sauce is a little thick, you can add a splash of water from the kettle, but be sure to note how that affects the flavour – you might need to back it up with a little more of the triumvirate of vinegar, sugar and salt. The final thing to note is that things taste stronger when they are warm than when they are cold. So take the seasoning of the sauce right up to its highest notes at this point. Once it is at room temperature and you are slathering it all over your chicken wings, we would hate for it to be underwhelming. And you could blend it until smooth here if you fancied! But we quite like it a bit gloopy. And! This is AMAZING mixed into yoghurt.

ROASTED GARLIC, CHIPOTLE & GRAVY SOUR CREAM

THIS LITTLE ADDENDUM TO THE MAYO SECTION IS FROM OUR SANDWICH 'THIS IS WHAT ARTHUR'S BEEF IS ALL ABOUT'. (PAGE 105) ARTHUR IS MY GODSON, THE CHILD OF MY DEAR FRIENDS KAT AND PAUL. I WENT TO PHOENIX, ARIZONA FOR HIS CHRISTENING AND CAME UP WITH THIS SANDWICH IN HIS HONOUR, FOR EVERYONE TO EAT AT THE PISS UP AFTERWARDS.

1 garlic bulb

Olive oil

8 large tbsps sour cream

4 tbsps beef gravy
(I'd made Barbacoa for
the sandwich in this
instance, but whatever
you might have)

2 scant tsps chopped up,
tinned chipotle peppers
(can sometimes be bought
in supermarkets or online)

(If you cooked Barbacoa
last night and are
sandwiching today, you
probably had chipotle in
the stew, so I'd ditch the
stuff in here. Might be a
bit much)

This is wicked simple to make but you need to do this first bit properly – it's the game changer.

Preheat your oven to 180°C.

Cut the garlic bulb in half, right across its middle, leaving all the cloves cut in half and exposed. Place the halves open side up on a baking tray and drizzle olive oil all over and leave it for a moment to soak in. Then drizzle olive oil all over it again. Put the tray in the oven for about 30 minutes (checking after 20).

You want the cloves to go as soft and golden as possible without burning. Once cooked and cooled a little, hold them by their bottoms and squeeze. The garlic will ooze out. Add that into the sour cream with the gravy and chipotle.

ANCHOVY SMOOSH

SOME PEOPLE CLAIM NOT TO LIKE ANCHOVIES. PAH!! THE SAME PEOPLE OFTEN LOVE THE RICH, UMAMI, SALT-BOMB OF ANCHOVY AND GARLIC IN THE BASE OF A SALSA VERDE OR COATING A SLOW-COOKED LAMB SHOULDER OF LAMB WITHOUT KNOWING ANCHOVIES ARE PART OF THE DEAL. DON'T BE A NINNY: MAKE THIS ANCHOVY SMOOSH AND ADD IT OCCASIONALLY TO A SANDWICH CONTAINING CRUNCHY BITTER VEGETABLES OR NAUGHTY RICH MEAT. YOU CAN THANK US LATER.

2 garlic cloves, grated

A small pinch of salt

8 anchovy fillets

Juice of ½ lemon

100ml extra virgin olive oil

8 turns of a pepper mill

You want to do this in a pestle and mortar. You will feel like an Italian grandmother and as such the resulting sauce will be even more delicious.

Start by adding the garlic and a small pinch of salt to the mortar. The salt is for traction rather than flavour so be sparing.

Start to grind the garlic with the pestle and as you do so, add the anchovies one at a time. When you have a unified fishy paste, add the lemon juice a little at a time and watch the paste turn from a murky brown to a pleasing caramel colour.

When the lemon juice is all incorporated, add the oil slowly as if for mayonnaise, working away with your pestle as you go. The mixture can split here, so do proceed with measured caution. Take your time to work the oil into the moosh. Once the oil is all in, add your pepper, taste with the end of your little finger, smile to yourself and go forth and slather it on anything and everything.

TAPENADE

THERE ARE TIMES IN A SANDWICH-MAKER'S LIFE WHEN THEY WANT SOMETHING BETWEEN THEIR BREAD THAT IS SALTY AND BITTER AND A LITTLE SHARP; SOMETHING TO COUNTER THE RICH, FATTY GOODNESS THAT THEY HAVE PILED UP READY TO DEVOUR. AT TIMES LIKE THIS, TAPENADE IS JUST THE THING.

4 anchovy fillets

2 garlic cloves, grated

1 tbsp capers, drained if in liquid and rinsed if in salt

Zest of 1 lemon and maybe some juice

½ tsp dried chilli flakes

A small bunch of parsley, leaves picked and stalks finely chopped

4 thyme sprigs, leaves picked, stalks discarded

200g pitted black olives

100ml extra virgin olive oil, plus extra if desired

Dust off your food processor.

Into the bowl of said machine, add the anchovy fillets, garlic, capers, lemon zest, dried chilli flakes and parsley stalks. Blitz until they are a sticky mess and then add the parsley leaves and thyme.

Drain the pitted olives and add to the mixer along with half the olive oil. Blitz again in short pulses so as to retain some texture to the sauce. Taste it.

You can add some lemon juice at this point if you want a little sharpness, but otherwise I suspect you will be feeling pretty smug.

If you want your sauce to be a little looser, add the other half of the oil; if not, don't.

This is so good with yoghurt in sandwiches! And an absolute classic with leftover lamb.

SALSA VERDE

THIS DECEPTIVELY SIMPLE SAUCE WILL DANCE A MERRY JIG ACROSS ANYTHING YOU PUT IN FRONT OF IT.

1 garlic clove, grated

6 anchovy fillets (optional)

1 tbsp capers, drained and rinsed

1 tbsp Dijon mustard

1 large bunch of parsley, leaves picked

½ bunch of dill, leaves picked

½ bunch of mint, leaves picked

½ bunch of tarragon, leaves picked

1 tbsp red wine vinegar

Juice of 1 lemon

250ml olive oil

Salt and pepper

We must ask a favour of you here. Please choose knife-based graft over ease and forgo the food processor. These poor herbs will bruise something rotten if not treated with a suggestion of respect.

Take your sharpest knife and chop together as finely as you can, the grated garlic, anchovies (if you are using them) and capers. Pile the herbs on top of this chopped smoosh and chop them all again as fine as you can. It should look more like a very finely chopped salad than the blended salsa verdes you see about.

Sweep all this into a mixing bowl, before stirring in the vinegar and lemon juice. Season with a little salt and pepper, then slowly whisk in the oil. At this juncture you will have a delicious, piquant, herby sauce. Taste as always, and adjust the salt and lemon as you see fit.

You want this to be nice and sharp, to cut through the rich fillings you should be having it with in your sandwich. It's just as good with meat and fish as it is with beans and on salad.

SALSA ROJO

MARCOS, AS THIS SAUCE IS KNOWN IN THE TRADE, IS A FIERY LITTLE TINKER. BENEFITING FROM THE INTENSE DEPTH THAT BURNING THE FUCK OUT OF PEPPERS, ONIONS AND TOMATOES WILL GIVE A DISH, AND THE SMOKY DELIGHT THAT CHIPOTLE BRINGS TO THE PARTY. MARCOS WILL CUT A LEGENDARY FIGURE IN ANY SANDWICH.

4 garlic cloves, unpeeled and whole

2 tomatoes, halved

2 jalapeños, topped and halved

½ red onion, peeled and thickly sliced

3 dried chipotle peppers (if you can only get tinned soft ones no worries)

½ bunch of coriander roughly chopped, stalks included

1 tsp salt

1 tbsp red wine vinegar

Preheat the oven to 250°C.

Lay out your garlic, tomatoes, jalapeños and red onion on a baking tray and place in the screaming hot oven. Cook for 15 minutes or until the surfaces of the veg are well and truly blackened.

Meanwhile, toast the chipotle peppers in a dry pan over a low heat until their smoky fragrance troubles your nostrils. Leave to cool for a few moments before tearing them open and knocking out their seeds. If you have tinned chipotles, which are all soft and lovely, skip to the next step.

Next, get the food processor out. Peel the garlic and add all your other burnt veg, toasted (or not, if they were canned) chipotles, coriander leaves and stalks, salt and red wine vinegar to the mixer and blitz with carefree abandon. You want to have a fiery but sweet sauce here, close to a dip.

Upon tasting, adjust the salt and vinegar accordingly. If you think it needs it, you can add a little sugar at the end if your tomatoes have you let you down with their own sweetness.

When combined with yoghurt or mayonnaise and some leftover stew or roast chicken or something in a sandwich this is gonna be off the hook.

SALSA ROMESCO

LIKE RICKY MARTIN IN LEATHER SHORTS, THIS SAUCE HAS SASS, VERVE AND RHYTHM. IN SPAIN THEY SERVE IT WITH MEAT, FISH, GRILLED VEG AND ESPECIALLY WITH GRILLED CALÇOTS, A LARGER-THAN-LIFE SPRING ONION. IT IS ALSO TRADITIONALLY MADE WITH ALMONDS IF YOU HAVE AN ALMOND TREE, OR BREAD, IF YOU DON'T. LUCKILY, WE CAN GO TO THE SUPERMARKET, SO WE'VE DONE IT WITH BOTH.

6 garlic cloves, skin on

6 large tomatoes
(about 500g), halved

2 red peppers, green bit removed, deseeded and cut into large pieces

4 tbsps extra virgin olive oil

1 tsp salt

40g stale bread, cut into 1cm cubes

40g blanched almonds

1 tsp hot smoked paprika

3 tsps red wine vinegar

Preheat the oven to 200°C.

In a large roasting tray, combine the garlic, halved tomatoes and chunks of red pepper and cover with one tbsp of oil and the tsp of salt. Place in the preheated oven and roast hard for 40 minutes until the skins of the vegetable are well and truly blackened.

While the veg is in the oven, lay out the bread cubes on a separate roasting tray and cover with two tbsp of oil, rubbing it in with your fingers gently massage the bread and whack it in the oven. These will need 5–10 minutes to become roasted and crispy. Some small burnt edges are OK, but watch it closely, you do not want a tray of burnt bread. When they're done, stick them in a bowl and clean the tray.

Stick the almonds on the tray and roast for 5 minutes, to start them colouring and get all the nice nutty oils going and to add a little roasted flavour.

Once you have three lots of variously roasted treats, you need to find a pestle and mortar or food processor.

Start by picking out and peeling the roasted garlic, add it to the mortar or food processor and pound/blitz it. Then add half the crispy bread cubes and nuts and blitz/pound until they are broken down but not too fine a powder. Next, add the peppers to the mix one by one, incorporating as you go. Finally add the tomatoes and mix into a nice rough sauce. As the veg are all well roasted, they should break down very easily.

Once you are happy, add the remaining bread, the paprika, the vinegar and a little more salt if you think it needs it. Mix well and taste, adjusting the seasoning as you see fit.

DILL PICKLE & TARRAGON SALSA

THIS IS SO GOOD WITH COLD ROAST MEATS AND PÂTÉ OF ALL KINDS. WE USE IT WITH WILD GARLIC ADDED WHEN IN SEASON, FOR OUR GUINEA FOWL SANDWICHES. AND I MAKE IT AT HOME AND HAVE IT WITH COLD 'LEFTOVER' ROAST CHICKEN IN A DREAMY LITTLE SANDWICH.

250g gherkins, coarsely grated

½ bunch of tarragon, stalks removed and leaves finely chopped

½ red onion, finely chopped or coarsely grated

2 heaped tsps Dijon mustard

25ml extra virgin olive oil

A big pinch of salt

Mix everything together. Slather on stuff and enjoy enormously.

MEERA'S CORIANDER, GREEN CHILLI & PEANUT CHUTNEY

WE HAVE OUR MIRACULOUS FRIEND MEERA SODHA TO THANK FOR THIS RECIPE. DO YOU REMEMBER THIS FROM THE BHAJI SMUGGLER ON PAGE 34? THE MILD HEAT AND SALTY-SOUR TANG OF THIS WONDERFUL SAUCE, MEAN THAT ALMOST ANYTHING TASTES GOOD ONCE THEY HAVE MET.

1 large bunch of coriander, leaves picked and stalks chopped

60g salted peanuts (not roasted)

2 decent green chillies sliced up (or 2 tbsps of jalapeño slices if you've got them in the fridge)

Juice of 2 limes

3 tsps sugar (brown ideally, but whatever you've got)

1 tsp ground turmeric

Start with a food processor. Add the coriander stalks, peanuts, ground turmeric, green chillies and sugar to the machine and blitz until they are firmly disciplined. Add the lime juice and the coriander leaves and blitz until you have a cohesive nutty looking sauce. Decant to a jar or bottle and store somewhere cold but within easy reach, like the fridge. Dunk anything in it.

LABNEH AND HER BEDFELLOW HARISSA

For the labneh:

500g Greek yoghurt

5g salt

For the harissa:

1 red pepper

3 red chillies, roughly chopped

1 tsp coriander seeds

1 tsp cumin seeds

1 tsp caraway seeds

2 tbsps olive oil

3 garlic cloves, grated

1 tsp tomato purée

Juice of 1 lemon

1 tsp Salt

Labneh:

Take a clean mixing bowl and a very clean cloth. A tea towel is ideal but it could be muslin, bed sheets or a beach towel. Lay the cloth flat and over the bowl.

In the tub you bought it in, mix the yoghurt with the salt. Then empty it into the middle of the cloth in the bowl. Next, collect the four corners of the cloth and bring them together. Liquid will flow out immediately. Twist the resulting hanging ball of cloth filled with yoghurt until you have a well-contained sphere. Leaving it in the bowl in case you drop it, tie the hanging strands of cloth in a knot and hang the yoghurty-amoeba in the fridge over a bucket or bowl to catch the liquid that will drip from your yoghurt-in-a-cloth. You will be surprised how much liquid comes out of it. In The Sandwich Shop we have a plate drying rack over the sink and we just tie it on to that so it drips straight into the sink.

After 4 hours or so, the yoghurt will have thickened perfectly. If you leave it out longer it will continue to thicken and become cheese-like, which is fine too, but we like this consistency. Now take the labneh out of the cloth, put it in a bowl, and put your cloth in the wash.

Harissa:

Turn on the gas hob on your cooker, or fire up your grill to its hottest setting if you don't have a gas cooker. Put the pepper and the chillies in the actual flames, actually in them, or under them if you've a grill and burn them until their skin is blistered and black all over, this should take three or four minutes a side. Look at the photo on p.161 that's what we're talking about. When you take the veg out of the flames, put it in a bowl immediately and clingfilm it over. The clingfilm will rise up and fall again over about 20 minutes as the hot veg steams, then cools. When it has cooled, you will be able to remove the skins easily.

Toast the coriander seeds, cumin seeds and caraway seeds in a dry pan over a medium flame. When you can smell the pleasant, not yet burnt smell of these spices, remove them from the pan, and grind them to dust in a food processor or pestle and mortar. Put the ground spices, the olive oil, grated garlic, tomato purée and lemon juice in a bowl and mix to a consistent sauce. Add some salt and check the seasoning.

Take the burnt pepper and chillies from the bowl, peel off their skins and discard their seeds. A spoon is often the best tool for this. Finely chop the soft flesh and add to the sauce. Mix well, slightly crushing the pepper and chilli into the sauce.

You now have labneh and harissa. And you are free to use them in your sandwiches independently of one another or together. Whether you lather this on bread soon to be topped with something tasty, or use it as a sauce to dip and dunk things into, you will be well pleased.

Burning the veg on a barbecue is always fun too. A good way to use the heat of the thing for something to be eaten another time.

i went ... max's sandwich shop and
all i got ... was this lousey
self promotion opportunity

PINE NUT TARATOR

THIS IS OUR LITTLE FRIEND FROM PAGE 73

200g pine nuts

1 garlic clove, grated

2 tbsps red wine vinegar

Juice of ½ lemon

120ml water

2 tbsps extra virgin olive oil

Salt

Find a blender or food processor. Add everything bar the salt. Blitz like a bad ass until smooth like body butter (1 full minute) Taste, season, and taste again.

In the sandwich from earlier in the book we used a nice pointy cabbage but this could done with purple sprouting broccoli, baby gem lettuces cut in half or a big broccoli 'tree' cut tip to toe into eighths and blanched in boiling water as the cabbage was (p.73), then slathered in this stuff.

If you are having a barbecue burn the veg while it is still too hot for the burgers or the sausages and make the sauce before you even light the barbie.

RAITA

IT'S A SAD DAY WHEN YOUR TAKEAWAY ISN'T GRACED BY AN OVERFLOWING STYROFOAM CUP OF SOOTHING RAITA, BUT IT DOES HAPPEN. SO MAKE SOME. SO SIMPLE, SO DELICIOUS. THE COOLING WONDERFUL FRIEND OF A SCORCHING HOT CURRY. AND IT'S SUCH A WONDERFUL THING IN A SANDWICH.

½ cucumber

¼ tsp salt

100g Greek yoghurt

½ tsp ground cumin

Juice of a ½ lemon

¼ bunch of fresh mint, leaves removed and chopped

Take the half a cucumber and cut it in half, then again and then again. You have eight pieces. Remove the seeds with your knife or a spoon and discard them. Then slice all the pieces into the thinnest tiniest slices you can. Put them in a bowl and stir in the salt.

Alternatively, instead of removing the seeds and cutting the cucumber up, you can just grate it as is on the coarse bit of your grater and put that in a bowl with the salt.

Both are delicious, but you will end up with a different sauce. Try both and see which you prefer.

Add the yoghurt, cumin and lemon juice to the cucumber and mix well. Taste, adjust the seasoning and then stir in the chopped mint. Voilà! You could cook the lamb curry on p.164, make some rice and have it with this and then put the whole bloody lot in a sandwich tomorrow? And don't forget Poppadoms. All this kind of thing needs crunch.

TOMATO SAUCE

THIS IS THE SIMPLEST TOMATO SAUCE YOU WILL EVER MAKE. IT IS ALSO THE BEST. AS SUCH, WE'RE GOING TO MAKE A LOT, AND YOU ARE GOING TO STORE IT IN SMALL CONTAINERS IN YOUR FRIDGE AND OR FREEZER.

1 tbsp extra virgin olive oil

2 garlic cloves, peeled and sliced

4 x 400g tins tomatoes, opened and ready

Salt

Dig out your heavy-bottomed saucepan and place it over a medium heat and warm the olive oil. Add the garlic and sizzle until you see it beginning to go golden. Immediately add the tinned tomatoes and all their tin juice. Fill one can up with water and swill this about in each can to capture any lurkers. Add this water to the pan.

Increase the heat and bring the sauce to a boil and then continue to boil (not simmer, boil) for about 20 minutes. The sauce should reduce by half. It will need regular stirring and maybe, the heat turning down, if it is boiling, and therefore reducing, too fast. We've added no salt yet.

Once you have reduced the sauce sufficiently, taste, add salt and taste again. Get it tasting mega and then leave it to sit and cool.

SWEET STICKY BBQ SAUCE

THERE IS NOT A MAN, WOMAN OR CHILD ON THIS PLANET WHO DOESN'T ENJOY A SWEET, STICKY BBQ SAUCE.

1 tbsp rapeseed oil

1 red onion, finely diced

1 garlic clove, grated

8 tbsps dark brown sugar

1 tsp salt

400ml passata

150ml white wine vinegar

½ tbsp ground black pepper

½ tbsp mustard powder

Juice of ½ lemon

3 tbsps Worcestershire sauce

1 tsp cayenne pepper

Take your heaviest bottomed saucepan and place it over a medium heat. Add the oil and allow it to get hot before putting in the onion, garlic, brown sugar and salt. Cook this for 8–10 minutes stirring pretty regularly. The sugar will make this go nice and dark, and the onions will sweat and caramelise too. This is good.

If you are ever worried they could begin to burn, just chuck a glug of water from the kettle in (hot, cold, doesn't really matter). It will always bubble away eventually but helps you keep things under control. We are often afraid of putting water in stuff, but it can always be boiled away. It is the cook's best friend, a splash of water.

Once you are happy that the onions are soft and sweet, increase the heat as high as it will go and add the vinegar. This should sizzle and spit, and you should scrape the bottom of the pan with your wooden spoon so all those dark tasty bits are incorporated back into the sauce.

Once the vinegar has all but reduced, add everything else. Stir well to combine, reduce the heat to its lowest possible setting and allow the sauce to simmer sleepily, bloop bloop, for the next 45 minutes, stirring very occasionally to watch for sticking.

The sauce should now be thick, and brown, and sweet. Taste it. If you like more heat, add cayenne; if you like more sweetness, add more sugar; if you like more sharpness, add more vinegar; if it tastes a little flat, add more salt. When it tastes nice, cool it in a bowl or jar before placing in the fridge and waiting for its moment to arrive.

TOMATO & CHARRED CORN SALSA

GOD BLESS SWEETCORN. AS WELL AS ALL IT'S NORMAL CHARMS YOU CAN ALSO BURN IT A BIT TO ENHANCE ITS SWEET AND DELICIOUS FLAVOUR. THIS SALSA COULD HAVE A KIND OF FRANKIE & BENNY'S FRIED PLATTER VIBE ABOUT IT, BUT IN THE RIGHT HANDS, IT BECOMES THIS AMAZING SALSA THAT A WIZENED MEXICAN GRANDMA MIGHT SERVE ON THE SIDE OF HER QUESADILLAS. WE SERVE IT WITH BARBACOA BEEF (PAGE 162) AND IT COULDN'T BE HAPPIER.

2 sweetcorn cobs, preferably with the ears (or leafy outside bits) still on

¼ red onion, chopped up tiny

2 ripe tomatoes, diced (skinned previously if you can be arsed (p.207), but don't stress)

1 jalapeño, finely sliced or chop up a tbsp of them pickled sliced ones

1 large handful of coriander leaves and stalks, finely chopped

Juice of 1 lime

A tbsp of fish sauce in here is well nice too, if you've got some kicking about

1 tsp salt

Start by getting a dry frying pan very hot over a high heat. Lay the corn, as god grew it, in the pan and cook, turning occasionally, until the ears are completely black, the extractor fan's given up and a neighbour's called the fire brigade. Remove the corn from the pan, peel back the outer leaves and discard. Lay the corn back in the pan and cook for 30 seconds on each side so that the kernels are a little blackened.

Stand the charred corn on a chopping board and carefully run a knife down each side of the corn to remove the kernels from the husk. Put these into a mixing bowl and add the onion, tomatoes, jalapeño and coriander. Toss well and season with the lime juice and salt. Taste. You want this sharp and fresh. So add a little more lime juice if needs be. When you are happy, combine in a sandwich with rich, smoky (barbacoa) meat, or simply shovel it towards your face with a tortilla chip or something similar.

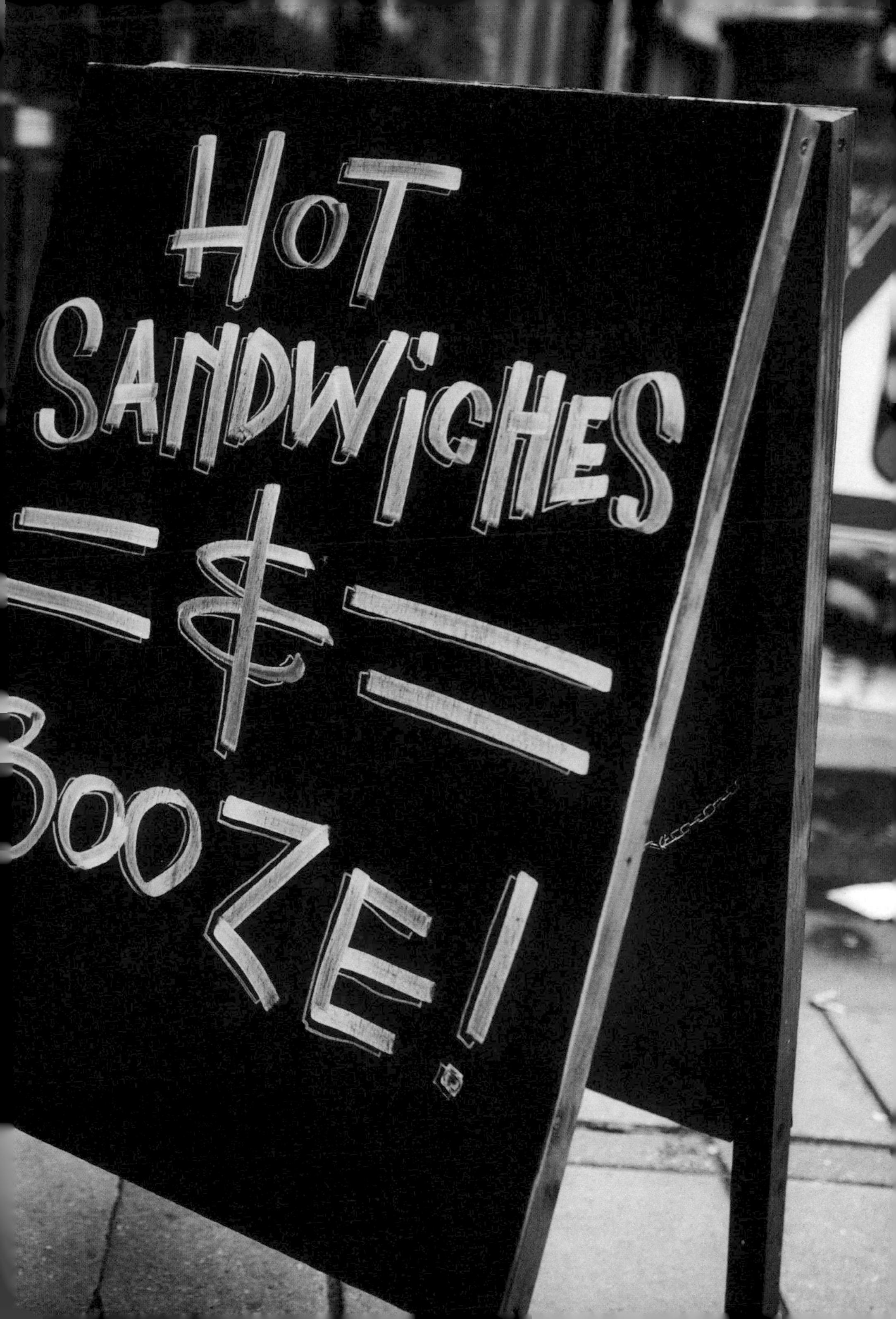
HOT SANDWICHES
&
BOOZE!

ROSE HARISSA YOGHURT

THIS IS POSSIBLY, APART FROM CHRAIN (BELOW), THE WORLD'S BEST CONDIMENT.

2 tbsps Greek yoghurt

1 tbsp rose harissa (courtesy of Belazu Fine Foods. It's stupidly expensive but it's genuinely delicious and will keep FOREVER in the fridge. Buy a tub – you are going to eat a lot of this)

Mix the harissa through the yoghurt. Dunk things that are tasty already in this yoghurt and close your eyes as your brain short circuits and sends sensory lightning rods through your body to your extremities. Dunk again, it never gets less exciting. I have it with roast chicken quite often! Chips from the chippie with this is fucking ridiculous!!!

You can marinade meat in it before you barbecue it. You can put it in an omelette. Have some on a fried egg. Whack it in a sausage sandwich. Its uses are verging on infinite.

CHRAIN, KING OF THE CONDIMENTS

Take one packet of cooked beetroot and put it in a blender with as much horseradish sauce as you like, which should be loads, or some of the grated (peeled) raw root itself if you can find one. Blend until smooth-ish. Add some wine vinegar and salt to taste.

There is very little in the world this isn't delicious with. Salt beef is a classic, anything fishy is brilliant, just give stuff a go.

WILD GARLIC SALSA

WILD GARLIC IS FREE. GOOGLE IT AND SEE WHAT IT LOOKS LIKE, NOW LOOK AT ANY DAMP VERGE ON ANY WET, WILD AND WINDY COUNTRY ROAD BETWEEN MARCH AND JUNE. WHEN YOU FIND IT, PICK SOME. IT TASTES LIKE GARLIC CROSSED WITH THE WORLD'S STRONGEST CHIVE, AND THAT IS GREAT. AND THE FLOWERS ARE WONDERFUL IN SALADS.

300g wild garlic leaves, chopped up a bit

1 tsp red wine vinegar

1 tsp Dijon mustard

Juice of ½ lemon

100ml extra virgin olive oil

Find a blender or a food processor. Add all your ingredients and blitz, keep blitzing, then taste. Do chop it all up before blending though, it goes quite stringy and I once burnt out a blender making it. Season with a little salt. Taste again. If the wild garlic is too dominant, add more mustard and more lemon juice until you are happy with the flavour. Now smear lavishly on anything you like.

Max's Sandwich Shop

FOR EATING IN OR TAKING AWAY

James' Amazing Kim Kong Kimchi & Kraut £2.50
Deep Fried Jalapeno Mac 'n' Cheese Balls £1.25 each

1. HAM, EGG 'N' CHIPS: £8.95
Slow cooked ham hock, a fried egg, piccalilli, shoestring fries, malt vinegar mayo

2. THIS IS HOW WE SPRING ROLL: £8.95
Dre's Pickled Spring Rolls, fresh ginger, coriander, parsley and mint, Kim Kong Kimchi, black and white sesame, black bean and MSG mayo

3. THE KOREAN GANGSTER: £8.95
Soy braised beef, Kim Kong Kimchi and Kraut, baby gem, parsley, deep fried noodles, incredibly slutty gravy and doenjang mayo

4. ET TU BRUTE? MURDERING THE CAESAR: £8.95
Roasted guinea fowl, pickled grape and tarragon salsa, baby gem, chicory, garlic croutons, anchovy mayo

OTHER TINGS:

SPUDS: A plate of crushed fried potatoes, curry powder and garam masala salt, lime pickle mayo, Bombay mix, spring onion, coriander and mint £4.50

TOM'S AMAZING WINGS: Soy and vinegar marinated chicken wings fried in Smash with guindilla yoghurt and lime pickled onions £5

PUDDING: Malt loaf crisps, chocolate and hazelnut ice cream, hazelnut butter, pomegranate molasses, vanilla salted caramel £6

Please tell us if you've got any allergies. Cheers

BEETROOT BORANI

I SWEAR DOWN THIS IS THE BESTEST THING EVER MADE WITH BEETROOT. SMEAR THIS ON BREAD AND YOU ARE TWO THIRDS OF THE WAY TO A MICHELIN STAR. YOU CAN'T SAY FAIRER THAN THAT.

1 of those vacuum packed cooked beetroot packs, juice and all

1 garlic clove, grated

½ a bunch of dill, bottom half of the stems finely chopped, top half roughly chopped

50ml extra virgin olive oil, plus extra for drizzling

100ml Greek yoghurt

2 handfuls of walnuts

2 tbsps red wine vinegar

50g feta cheese

Find a food processor. Put the walnuts in and blitz them thoroughly first. Add the beetroots (with all the juice from the pack) and the garlic and give it 4-5 cursory pulses. Add the dill stalks and blitz like a banshee. Add everything else and return to your cursory pulses until you have a nice smooth, bright pink smoosh. Taste it. If you want a bit more salt, add a few extra crumbles of feta. If you want it sharper, maybe add a little extra yoghurt or vinegar, or both.

Smear it on bread and top with more feta, perhaps a croqueta or two (p.202), some herbs and a sharp and peppery salad. As we mentioned previously, you can assume a Michelin Star will be on its way via recorded delivery. This is in Ben's guest sandwich from The Sandwich Shop, The BJ Benton (p.42) but we don't put the cheese in because I'm funny about feta. We just use salt to do the same thing. But of course, do whatever you think is more delicious.

GUINDILLA YOGHURT

I worked for Brindisa (Britain's top (and best!) Spanish food importer) at the beginning of my career in this food lark. They are the best Spanish food importer in the business. Hands down. I don't know if they still can, but they used to be able to say they sold food to every Michelin-starred restaurant in Britain. I stopped working for them in 2008 and they still ask me to their parties. They're a joy. Abi and Cristina, James, Monika and, of course my dear dear friend Rudi Von Vollmar are all at the top of their game.

We buy their hot guindillas (pickled peppers) and blend huge handfuls of them, with some of the liquid from the jar and mix the paste into yoghurt to go on our Chicken Wings (p. 252). They're a posher version of those chillies from the kebab shop and they're delicious. Especially with Manzanilla or Fino sherry, some cured pork loin and the company of your friend Ben Falk on a sunny afternoon at home bunking off work and looking at the fish tank.

LIME PICKLE YOGHURT

We make this sauce for going on our deep fried spuds. We buy lime pickle from the corner shop, get whichever one is your favourite, put it in a blender and blitz it until it's smooth. Then mix it into low fat yoghurt. We use low fat yoghurt for this because it's much runnier than full fat so it coats the spuds better.

FLAVOURED BUTTERS

You do not have to refrigerate butter. It is still (just) a solid at room temperature and it's much easier to mix things into it when it's in this soft state. It can always be put back in the fridge post-combining and firmed up again. Good old butter.

Nearly anything you might put into mayonnaise, can be mixed into butter. Dry things like spices, very finely chopped/blitzed up herbs, condiments, the list goes on.

I love Tabasco and Lea & Perrins mixed together for toast and crumpets. My girlfriend, Holly Chaves, loves blending anchovies in there. You could buy some Gentleman's Relish and whack a load of that in. You get the idea.

MEAT

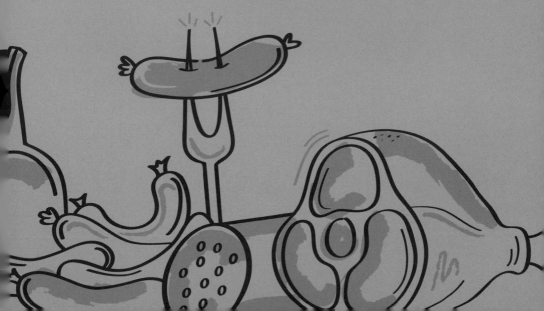

SLOW COOKED HAM HOCKS

THIS IS THE HAM FROM THE SANDWICH THAT STARTED IT ALL, THE HAM, EGG 'N' CHIPS (PAGE 26). IT IS ALSO THE RECIPE FOR A HAM HOCK THAT WOULD STAND UP AGAINST ANY PIECE OF COOKING YOU'D FIND ANYWHERE. YOU COULD FILL A MIND-BENDING PIE, OR SERVE THE HOCK AS IT IS WITH MASHED POTATO, AND SOME SAUERKRAUT AND MUSTARD. YOU COULD SET THE PICKED MEAT IN A TERRINE WITH PISTACHIOS AND PICKLED VEGETABLES. YOU COULD WIN A MICHELIN STAR. DO WHAT YOU WANT ONCE YOU'VE MADE THE RECIPE, JUST PROMISE US YOU WILL MAKE THE RECIPE.

2½kg ham hocks (which is probably 2 and we prefer unsmoked at The Sandwich Shop)

3 celery stalks, cut into 3 pieces each

2 carrots unpeeled, split in half

1 large white onion, peeled and cut in half

75ml cider vinegar (or white wine vinegar)

Leftover (red or white) wine

1 tsp coriander seeds (don't bother roasting them)

2 tsps whole black peppercorns

1 bunch of parsley, stalks and all

6 bay leaves, dried or nicked from the neighbour's garden

In a large, heavy-bottomed saucepan, put the bunch of parsley at the bottom and place the ham hocks, celery, carrots, and onion and bay leaves on top. Cover with the cider vinegar (and the wine/cider if you have it) and enough water to just submerge the meat. Lob in the coriander seeds and peppercorns. Cover with a cartouche (p.158) and bring to a boil. Reduce the heat to maintain the gentlest of simmers and cook for 1½ hours, or until the ham falls easily off the bone. Sometimes this might take 2 hours, it's a bastard.

Drain (by putting a colander in a big bowl or another saucepan in the sink), reserving the liquid for soup, if you like, but importantly for tipping onto the meat when you have picked it from the bones and skins and removed any shifty looking bits.

When the ham is cool enough to handle, pick it from the bones and separate out the skins, discarding the bones. Put the meat in a Tupperware or bowl or something and tip cooking liquid onto the meat, just enough to cover it. It will turn to jelly and look weird after it's been in the fridge but it'll all melt and be lush when you make the sandwich.

If you are feeling like a kitchen ninja, you can keep the skin to make scratchings (see recipe on p.173), but if not, fuck it, bin it.

BRAISED BEEF FOR ALL SEASONS

"IF YOU DON'T KNOW, NOW YOU KNOW" – NOTORIOUS B.I.G (BEEF. IN. GRAVY)

DON'T BE PUT OFF MAKING THIS RECIPE BECAUSE IT APPEARS TO HAVE A LONG LIST OF INGREDIENTS. YOU START BY BURNING STUFF, AND WE CAN ALL DO THAT (PAGE 161) AND FOLLOW BY SPLASHING A LOAD OF STUFF INTO A TRAY, WHICH IS WHACKED IN AN OVEN FOR 5 HOURS. TREAT YOURSELF TO A BOTTLE OF WINE OR SOMETHING.

2½kg braising steak, from the butcher if you can, or beef shin or oxtail

1 onion

2 carrots

5cm piece of ginger

1 whole garlic bulb

1 x 400g tin of chopped tomatoes

2 tbsps doenjang (fermented soya bean paste – Korean miso)

250ml white wine vinegar

125ml light soy sauce

125ml dark soy sauce

50ml fish sauce

75g caster sugar

1 x 330ml can of stout, like Guinness

Enough water to cover

Preheat the oven to 120°C.

Burn, really burn, the veg whole and unpeeled, even the onion and the garlic. (p.161) You can do this in the gas flames of your cooker if you have them, otherwise under the grill.

Throw the burnt veg, even the ashy looking suspicious bits, and all your other ingredients into a large flameproof casserole or oven-safe saucepan. Place it over a high heat on your stove, cover with a cartouche (p.158) and bring to the boil. Put the lid on. If your giant pot has no lid, as some don't, foil pinched round the perimeter of the pan will be fine. But still use the cartouche. And use two layers of foil, then put it in the oven and cook for 5 hours.

Remove from the oven, uncover and allow to cool enough so that you can put your hands in. Take the meat out, pick it from the bones if there are any, and throw them away. Put the meat in a suitable container. Cover it in enough of the cooking liquor to submerge it. Sieve the rest of the cooking liquid into a pan, throw the veg away and boil down the liquid to make a thick gravy – the thicker the better (around ⅛ of its original volume. It will be much thicker cold than it is hot). This treacle-like gravy will keep for months in the fridge. Promise. And can be heated up for mixing into mayo whenever you like (see Gravy Mayo recipe on p.125).

To reheat the meat for sandwiching, just put some in a saucepan with the now jelly-like juice it's been kept in and a splash of water, and heat until piping hot.

You could just have this as a stew with mash potato and some cabbage. And what a sandwich you will have for your dinner tomorrow.

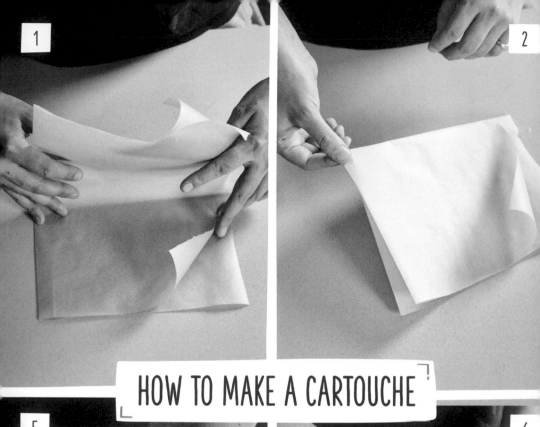

HOW TO MAKE A CARTOUCHE

WITH BAKING PAPER

GANGNAM SHORT RIBS

THE INTERNATIONAL POP SENSATION PSY ATE THESE EXACT RIBS FOR LUNCH FOR 912 DAYS STRAIGHT,
(THAT'S TWO AND A HALF YEARS!), AND THAT IS A TRUE FACT.

2½kg beef short ribs

2 red onions, halved but unpeeled

1 bunch of spring onions

2 tomatoes

2 red peppers

1 garlic bulb

2 x 5cm pieces of ginger

1 tbsp Salt

1 lemongrass stick, whacked and bruised with the back of a knife

Water

4 tbsps soy sauce

2 tbsps honey

1 tbsp toasted sesame oil

1 small bunch of coriander, leaves picked from the stalks, stalks finely chopped

Preheat the grill.

Load your onions, spring onion, whole tomatoes, whole peppers, garlic and whole ginger into a roasting tray and place under the grill. If you don't have a grill, you'll need to do this in the flames of your gas hob or on a barbecue, but there will be a little bit of cleaning up to do afterwards. You want to burn this veg until it is well and truly black. Keep checking on it and remove the veg as and when it is burnt to perfection. Do not try and peel it or wash it – you want all that burnt goodness. You will smell how good this is going to taste right from this first stage. Burning veg is rather unexpectedly, one of the most wonderful smells there is.

Once all your veg is burnt, turn your oven to 120°C. Next, combine the burnt veg with the short ribs and the rest of the ingredients in a roasting tray large enough to hold everything. The only thing to hold back is the coriander leaves. The stalks can go right in. Now add water until everything is completely covered.

Cover as always with a cartouche (p.158) and two layers of foil, and place in the oven for 2½ hours. The short ribs should be soft and the meat should fall away easily when you pick the bone up. Allow the meat to cool before picking it from the bones.

Strain the sauce through a sieve, and taste – it should be bloody delicious. And after you've slathered some on your ribs for your tea, the rest of it should definitely be reduced further in a saucepan and be mixed into mayonnaise later (see p.125 for the recipe for Gravy Mayo).

BARBACOA BEEF

THIS SHIT IS DARK, SMOKY, MYSTERIOUS AND SEXY AS HELL. WE USED THIS RECIPE FOR THE BEEF IN THE SANDWICH WE MADE CALLED 'THIS IS WHAT ARTHUR'S BEEF IS ALL ABOUT' (PAGE 105). ARTHUR IS MY GODSON AND THE CHILD OF MY FRIENDS KAT AND MERRY. THEY LIVE IN PHOENIX, ARIZONA AND ASKED ME TO MAKE A SANDWICH FOR THE POST-CHRISTENEING PARTY WHICH I DID, AND IT WAS ON THE MENU AS SOON I WAS BACK IN THE SANDWICH SHOP.

AS PER USUAL, IF YOU ARE GOING TO GO TO ALL THIS TROUBLE, GO BIG. YOU'LL EAT IT EVENTUALLY, TRUST US.

2kg braising steak cut into large chunks

2 tbsps rapeseed oil

2 jars chipotle adobo or chipotle paste (you can find it in some supermarkets, online might be easier)

A bunch of coriander, stalks removed and finely chopped, leaves roughly chopped

1 red onion, burnt whole, then quartered with the skin on

1 whole garlic bulb, halved and burnt over an open flame (Read p.160 for burning skills)

5 cloves

5 bay leaves

1 tbsp sea salt

4 limes, halved, open face burnt in a dry, incredibly hot frying pan,

100ml red wine vinegar

Water

Dig out a heavy-bottomed, lidded saucepan large enough to all fit your beef and goodies in. Place this over a medium flame. Warm the oil and then fry the chipotle paste until your nostrils are twitching.

Add the coriander stalks, onion, garlic, cloves and bay leaves and fry for a few minutes in the chipotle and oil. Season your beef with the sea salt and add this to the pot.

Squeeze the burnt limes and add both the juice and the fruit to the pot. Add the vinegar and the water, making sure the beef is just about covered. If it isn't, more water. Bring to the boil and then immediately turn down the heat to the lowest it will go. Cover with a cartouche (p.158). Leave to gently blip away for 5 hours, until the meat falls apart when prised between two fingers. Peek under the cartouche, now and again. Bit dry? Add some water from the kettle and keep cooking. Allow to cool before stirring though the coriander leaves.

Once cooked and cooled, remove the meat from the sauce (temporarily) and tear it into a pile. Lay this out on a baking tray and put in a searingly hot (250°C) oven for 10 minutes to crisp up and slightly burn it. Then fold this supercharged Barbacoa back through the delicious sauce and pile it high in a sandwich with some finely sliced radish, cabbage and sour cream.

Have a look at the 'This Is What Arthur's Beef Is All About' on p.105 to see what we put with this at The Sandwich Shop.

SEVEN-HOUR LAMB SHOULDER

GUESS HOW LONG THIS TAKES TO COOK?

IT'S LIKE THAT MOVIE *SINK THE BISMARCK*! GUESS WHAT HAPPENED?

THIS LITTLE TINKER HAS A REAL MIDDLE EASTERN SWING TO IT, AND LIKE MOST OF OUR MEAT DISHES, IT'S EASY TO DO AND REWARDS A PROPENSITY TOWARDS CHILLING THE FUCK OUT. YOU'RE WELCOME.

1 lamb shoulder, roughly 2kg, taken out the fridge at least 1 hour before cooking

1 whole garlic bulb, chopped in half

3 onions, halved with the skins still on

1 tbsp rapeseed oil

1 tbsp salt

2 tsps ground cumin

2 tsps dried chilli flakes

75ml pomegranate molasses

100ml red wine vinegar

In a roasting tray large enough to house the lamb shoulder, place the halves of garlic and onions face down – these are going to hold up the lamb shoulder from the base of the tray and help it cook evenly.

Preheat the oven to as hot as it goes.

Rub the lamb shoulder with the oil, then the salt, cumin and chilli flakes. Place the shoulder on top of the onions and garlic drizzle the molasses all over, then add the vinegar and 100ml of water to the tray.

Cover with a layer of baking paper and two layers of foil and place in the hot oven. Immediately turn the heat down to 100°C and leave in the oven for 7 hours.

When cooked, remove from the oven and allow to cool a bit. Lift the now pretty tender and soft, lamb shoulder from the tray. Pick the meat off in nice chunks. Reserve the sauce in the tray for putting on the meat on your plate, or in a sandwich. And keep a bit aside for mixing into mayo too.

CURRIED LAMB

NEVER SAY WE HAVEN'T GIVEN YOU VALUE FOR MONEY. THIS LAMB CURRY RECIPE WILL BLOW MINDS LEFT, RIGHT AND CENTRE. SERVE TO YOUR GUESTS WITH RICE, OUR RAITA (PAGE 142), LOADS OF WHOLE RAW SPRING ONIONS CUT INTO THIN SLICES (2 PER PERSON) AND SOME FLATBREADS.

SIMILARLY, THE NEXT DAY, WHEN LATHERED IN A SANDWICH WITH THE SAME RAITA, SOME LIGHTLY PICKLED ONIONS (PAGE 233) AND SHIT LOADS OF HERBS, YOU WILL HAVE SOMETHING OF BRUTAL DELIGHT ON YOUR HANDS. IF YOU CAN'T BE BOTHERED TO BUY ALL THE SPICES LISTED BELOW, JUST PURCHASE A GOOD GARAM MASALA – WE WON'T JUDGE YOU.

500g lamb shoulder, chopped into 2cm cubes

4 tbsps veg oil

2 white onions, chopped into the tiniest pieces you can manage

1 peeled carrot, as above

4 garlic cloves, grated

Index finger sized piece of ginger, peeled and grated

1 bunch of coriander leaves picked (to use later) and stalks finely chopped

2 green chillies, finely chopped, seeds and all

2 bay leaves

1 tsp ground cumin

1 tsp ground coriander

2 cloves

10 cardamom pods, smashed open

1 tsp fennel seeds

1 tsp chilli powder

1 cinnamon stick

2 tsps ground turmeric

2 tbsps red wine vinegar

1 x 400g tin tomatoes

2 tbsps ground almonds

2 tbsps Greek yoghurt

Find a massive heavy-bottomed saucepan and place it over a medium heat and warm the oil. Brown off the meat 6 or 7 chunks at a time and put them on a plate. Once they're all done, add a big slug more oil and scrape the bottom of the pan all over to get at the lovely bits. Add the onions, carrot, garlic, chillies, ginger and coriander stalks with a big pinch of salt. Cook for 15–20 minutes stirring occasionally and making sure not to overly colour everything. If you ever feel the pan is a bit dry and things are almost burning, not frying softly, add a bit more oil and lower the heat. Do not skimp on time here – those sweet onions are going to make this curry amazing.

Next, add the bay leaves and all the spices (or 2 generous tablespoons of your garam masala) and cook out until the scent of the spices is filling the kitchen. Next, increase the heat a notch or two and put the meat and all its juices back in the pan. Stir this through the spiced onions et al and allow it all to get going.

Add the vinegar and let it sizzle and spit in the pan. Cook it nearly completely away and then add the tomatoes (including all the tin juice and a bit of water swilled in the tin to get all the goods out), the ground almonds and the yoghurt. If you need some water to make sure the lamb is completely covered, add it from a boiled kettle. Bring the curry back to the boil and then immediately reduce the heat considerably and let it blob, blob, blob, away for an hour or so. Depending on the tenderness of the lamb it could take up to two hours, but you'll know it's ready when the lamb falls apart when prised between two fingers. If the lamb stays chewy for a while and the liquid seems to be leaving you too fast, just add more water from the kettle and reduce it slowly away again.

All you need to do at the end is stir through the coriander leaves and check your seasoning. And sort the other stuff (raita, rice etc.) out too. Sorry. Of course, curries can be and often are, made day(s) in advance.

And never forget, if you order enough, you can order just naans from your local Indian takeaway/restaurant.

BACON AT HOME

SOME PRIOR WARNING. THIS WILL TAKE A LONG TIME. YOU WILL NEED TO SACRIFICE SOME SPACE IN YOUR FRIDGE. YOU WILL WONDER WHY YOU ARE BOTHERING WITH THIS. THEN YOU WILL BECOME ADDICTED TO IT AND YOUR BACON SARNIE WILL NEVER BE THE SAME AGAIN.

2½kg pork belly, deboned, skin on

100g curing salt, from the internet, or sometimes the butcher will sell it to you

50g caster sugar

3 bay leaves

2 rosemary sprigs, leaves picked

1 tbsp black peppercorns

Before you start, find a resealable polythene bag large enough to fit the pork belly inside. Also, find a roasting tray large enough to fit this bag and belly in. And clear a space in your fridge large enough for the tray.

Blitz the curing salt, sugar, bay leaves, rosemary and black peppercorns in a food processor or spice grinder until it's a uniform powder. Place this mix in the plastic bag and add the pork belly. Seal the bag, ensuring you have squeezed out as much air as possible, and shake well so that the belly is completely covered in the salt cure. Massage a little to ensure you have a good coating.

Place this in the roasting tray and then in the fridge. Check the pork every day for the next 5 days, turning it and rubbing in the curing mix every day and pouring off any excess liquid. On the sixth day, remove the pork and discard the contents of the bag. Rinse the pork under cold water until all the cure mix has been washed away. Pat completely dry, wrap in a large tea towel, then place it on a meat hook and hang it to dry in a cool place, such as a cellar, larder or a cool garage. This is the air drying bit, and you can go as long as you like, but 2 or 3 days should suffice to begin with.

You now have your own "green" bacon. Do not be alarmed if a white mould appears; it's harmless, just rub it off. You are now free to slice and fry nice thick slabs of home-cured bacon and add them to your sandwiches. Please also feel free to use this bacon in any and every way you can imagine. Oh, and also, start a second batch once the first one is ready – you're going to want to keep some of this in stock.

When you are slicing your bacon, use your sharpest knife and put the belly skin side down on the chopping board, cutting through the meat down toward the skin. From behind is the best way through its toughness and will make it much easier to cut slices. As time goes by and the bacon cures more, this will become easier and easier as the meat firms.

Very occasionally, the whole bloody thing goes inexplicably horribly wrong and the bacon goes green in a bad way and goes off and all your time will have been wasted. God's a bastard. Try again.

Don't forget to cut the top layer of the skin off your slices of bacon when you cut it. You can bake these until golden and crispy, in a 180°C oven.

PORCHETTA

SOME PEOPLE SWEAR PORK BELLY MUST BE USED FOR THIS. THEY KNOW NOTHING. SHOULDER EVERY TIME.

2½kg deboned and rolled pork shoulder, skin on (this is crucial) and scored (you can ask your butcher to score the skin for you)

2 tbsps salt

1 tbsp fennel seeds

1 tbsp dried chilli flakes

6 garlic cloves, grated

3 rosemary sprigs, leaves picked, stalk chucked out

3 thyme sprigs, leaves picked, stalks chucked out

½ bunch of parsley

½ bunch of oregano or marjoram

100ml white wine

A ball of string

Preheat the oven to 200°C

Unfurl the pork shoulder of any string the butcher's put on it and lay it out flat, skin-side down. Pound (in a mortar) or blend (in a food processor) the salt, fennel seeds and chilli flakes before liberally sprinkling the pork with the mix.

Put the grated garlic on a chopping board, all the herbs on top and chop them all roughly together. Scatter this all over the seasoned pork.

Next, the (re)tying. Roll the shoulder tightly and tie a piece of string around one end, as tight as you can. Make a granny-knot, snip any spare off and move two inches down and do the same again and again. Repeat until you reach the end. You should now have a tied, sausage-shaped roll of pork. Plonk this in a roasting tray and pour in the wine.

Place the tray in the hot oven and cook for 30 minutes before turning the oven down to 160°C and cooking for a further 3-4 hours. Check the porchetta frequently and if the tray is dry, add a little water and if it's swimming in liquid, tip some away (but keep it for later).

Once the porchetta is cooked and a tug at a strand of meat has it pulling away from the roll, and the crackling has crackled, allow it to cool before slicing into 1cm thick rounds and serving it in your sandwich. It is just as delicious cold as it is warm.

You could also eat this with potatoes, salsa verde and a nice sauce made by reducing the leftover cooking liquid in a saucepan.

If you feel the pork has cooked and the crackling hasn't. Pop the whole thing under the grill tray and all. Keep an eye on it though. It's seconds from done to burnt.

MEATBALLS

A MEATBALL SUB...WHAT A CLASSIC...(PAGE 98)

WHAT FOLLOWS IS, FIRST OF ALL, A METHOD FOR MAKING SENSATIONAL MEATBALLS, AND A RECIPE FOR A CLASSIC ITALIAN-STYLE BEEF POLPETTE. THERE IS ALSO A LIST OF FURTHER COMBINATIONS THAT WORK PERFECTLY. THE BREADCRUMBS AND MILK MAKE THE MEATBALLS UNEXPECTEDLY LIGHT AND THE EGG BINDS THEM TOGETHER. THE SEASONING SHOULD BE ROBUST WITH SALT AND TWO FURTHER FLAVOURINGS – ANY MORE AND YOU RISK CONFUSING THE FLAVOUR OF THE BALLS. ALWAYS BUY THE BEST MINCE YOU CAN AND PLACE A PREMIUM ON HIGH FAT CONTENT AS THIS KEEPS THE BALLS JUICY AND NOT DRY.

Classic polpette

400g minced beef

200g minced pork or a large sexy sausage or two removed from their skins

60g (stale bread, if you have it, otherwise fresh, torn into scraps)

60ml milk

1 egg

30g Parmesan cheese, grated

¼ nutmeg, grated

2 tsps salt

Soak the bread scraps in the milk for 10 minutes. Meanwhile, mix the minced beef and pork with the rest of the ingredients and knead everything together. Finally, add the sodden bread and give the mixture one final knead. Shape the mixture into even sized "ping pong ball-ish" meatballs.

Roll one ball and fry it in some oil to test the seasoning. Adjust with salt as necessary. When you are happy, fry the rest off in a little oil so that they are brown on all sides and just cooked through.

Classically, these would then be simmered gently in some rich tomato sauce for 10–15 minutes (p.143) and eaten with linguine.

MORE MEATBALLS

WE THOUGHT WE'D GIVE YOU THESE OTHER BANGING MEATBALL RECIPES, SO THAT YOU CAN MAKE THEM, AND COME UP WITH MEATBALL SUB INVENTIONS OF YOUR OWN.

FOR EACH OF THESE FOLLOW THE RECIPE ON THE PREVIOUS PAGE FOR CLASSIC POLPETTE BUT OMIT THE RICH TOMATO SAUCE STAGE.

Spanish albondigas	Greek keftedes
60g stale bread, torn into scraps	60g stale bread, torn into scraps
60ml milk	60ml milk
300g minced beef	300g minced beef
300g minced pork	300g minced lamb
1 egg	1 egg
1 garlic clove, grated	2 garlic cloves, grated
1 tsp hot smoked paprika	1 handful of mint or oregano leaves, finely chopped
2 tsps salt	2 tsps salt

Asian chicken meatballs

60g stale bread, torn into scraps

60ml milk

600g minced chicken

1 egg

Thumb-sized piece of ginger, peeled and grated

2 tsps ground chilli flakes

2 tsps soy sauce

Lamb meatballs

60g stale bread, torn into scraps

60ml milk

600g minced lamb

1 egg

Zest of 1 lemon

1 handful of mint, finely chopped

2 tsps salt

BOLOGNESE À LA ROBERT CARRIER

THIS IS THE SIMPLEST MOST DELICIOUS BOLOGNESE RECIPE THERE IS. IT WILL FEED FOUR PEOPLE AND LEAVE ENOUGH FOR MAJOR LEFTOVER ACTION. YOU CAN FREEZE SOME, YOU CAN LASAGNE SOME, YOU CAN WHACK IT IN SARNIES OR HAVE IT ON TOAST WITH A FRIED EGG, HELL, MY DAD SOMETIMES EVEN MAKES RISOTTO WITH IT. THIS RECIPE BELONGS TO ROBERT CARRIER AND SIR, WE THANK YOU FOR IT (HE'S DEAD).

4 tbsps extra virgin olive oil

1kg minced beef
(buy the best you can buy,
visit your butcher)

6 slices of smoked streaky
bacon, thinly sliced

2 large onions,
finely chopped

2 large carrots, peeled,
cut in four length ways
and finely chopped

2 hefty celery stalks, cut in
four lengthways and finely
chopped

2 bay leaves, dried or
pinched from someone's
garden

1 vegetable peeler strip of
lemon peel

1 good pinch of
ground nutmeg

2 x 140g tins of tomato purée

1 litre (1½ stock cubes will
do) beef stock

Find a large heavy-bottomed pan. A casserole would be perfect here. Place the pan over a medium heat and get the olive oil in. Once the oil is hot, add the bacon and move it around with your wooden spoon. Once it's browned a bit (3/4 minutes), add the onion, carrot and celery. Add a good 4-finger pinch of salt, give it all a healthy stir and sweat out for 15 minutes, stirring occasionally. Do not skimp on this. That bacony residue and the long, slow sweating of your onions etc. will give you all the depth of flavour and sweetness this sauce needs. No cheeky addition of sugar here my friend (we're looking at you, Yotam).

After 15 minutes, increase the heat and add the mince. Cook until none of it is red any more and some bits are browning. Add the tins of tomato purée. Put some of your beef stock in the empty purée tins and swill it all about – leave no flavour stone unturned.

Add the stock filled tins, the rest of the stock, the lemon peel, the bay leaves and the nutmeg. Bring to the boil and reduce to a slow simmer. Put the lid on and don't touch it much – just checking occasionally that the bottom isn't sticking and lowering the heat if necessary.

After half an hour, take the lid off, remove the peel and bay and cook at the same gentle pace for at least 45 minutes more.

Tend it occasionally and regularly at first to make sure nothing's sticking, you might need to lower the heat a bit. There's never any harm in a cursory stir, a little taste. The liquid will reduce considerably and oil will rise to the surface, and your sauce will be ready.

SCRATCHINGS

WHEN WE COOK MEATS, WE LIKE TO USE ALL OF WHAT WE COOK. SO AFTER WE'VE BRAISED HAM HOCKS, WE LIKE TO NICK THE SKIN AND TURN IT INTO CRACKLING/SCRATCHINGS. CONFIT-ING SOME DUCK LEGS, OR POACHING A CHICKEN? GRAB THAT SKIN, STRETCH IT OUT AND BAKE IT. NOT ONLY DO YOU HAVE SOMETHING THAT CAN BE LABELLED COQ SCRATCHINGS OR FOWL SCRATCHINGS AND ILLICIT A SNIGGER, BUT YOU'LL HAVE SOMETHING SALTY AND DELICIOUS THAT WILL GIVE YOU ALL THE TEXTURE AND CRUNCH YOU NEED IN AN OTHERWISE SOFT SANDWICH.

This is not a recipe as such.

If you are going to make scratchings, it is best to remove the skin from your piece of meat before you cook it. In the case of something like porchetta (p.168), leave the skin on – it will naturally crisp.

Next, you want to dry the skin. So, lay it out as flat as possible on a wire rack on a baking tray and scatter it liberally with coarse sea salt. Place this in the fridge and leave for 4 hours or overnight. When ready to cook, pat dry with a paper towel, leaving the skin on the rack, and place into a preheated oven at 140°C. Depending on the type of skin you are turning into scratchings, and the fat content of said skin, the timing will vary, but start checking on it after about 15 minutes. It might take up to 40 minutes. You want nice brown crunchy skin so turn the tray round occasionally to avoid it burning in any hot spots in the oven.

When looking perfect, remove from the oven and allow to cool on the rack. If you are a fiend for salt and/or spices, it is best to sprinkle them on while the skins are still hot. At The Sandwich Shop we use a 50/50 mix of cumin powder and salt to sprinkle on the guinea fowl skins we make scratchings from. Don't forget that you have already salted your skins though (in order to dry them). When cool, you can snuffle these to your heart's content but do leave some for adding crunch to a sandwich that's begging for it.

BREADED MEATS

YOU CAN BREAD PRETTY MUCH ANY MEAT. THE RECIPE THAT FOLLOWS IS FOR THE BREADING AND THE COOKING. WE WILL LEAVE THE MEAT TO YOU. PORK, CHICKEN AND VEAL ARE THE CLASSICS, AND WE WOULD GENERALLY STICK TO THEM, BUT OF COURSE, GIVE ANYTHING YOU LIKE A GO!

This recipe is for breading two relatively large escalopes:

3 tbsps plain flour

2 tsps Salt

2 tsps ground black pepper

2 medium eggs

2 tbsps full fat milk

1 tbsp rapeseed oil

25g unsalted butter

50g dried white breadcrumbs (see Ned Halley's Breadcrumbs on p.218 or buy some panko ones, or get some from the baker)

Lay out a big bit of good quality cling film on your work surface. This sounds RIDICULOUS but cling film, is not cling film. There is good and bad. If yours is real cheap, it'll break too easily and this will be a nightmare. Put your bit of chicken breast or pork tenderloin or whatever you are 'Schnitzelling' on one side of the cling film and fold the other half over leaving plenty of plastic all round. Bash your meat violently to about 5mm thick with the base of a small saucepan. Bashing it thin will allow you to cook the meat thoroughly in the time it takes you to get the breadcrumbs a nice golden brown colour.

Find two bowls with a decent rim and one plate. In one of the bowls mix the flour, salt and pepper. In the second bowl whisk the eggs and the milk, and on the plate, spread the breadcrumbs.

Take your pounded meat and dust in the seasoned flour, knocking any excess off. Next, lay in the egg mixture and coat well on both sides. Finally, lay on the breadcrumbs plate and scoop them all over the escalope (schnitzel). If you are a glutton for thick crunchy breading, repeat the egg and breadcrumb steps a second time. You will not regret it, but it is not essential.

Get your best (thickest-based) frying pan and place over a low heat to get hot. After a few moments, add the oil and then butter to the pan and allow it to froth. Next, fry the escalopes one at a time for 3 minutes on each side. Do not be tempted to increase the heat as there is nothing worse after all this work than a burnt schnitzel. Having turned the meat and cooked it for another 3 minutes, remove to a plate with paper towel beneath it. Fry the next one.

These can go into a sandwich hot or cold, whole or sliced. And they are at their best with iceberg lettuce, mayo, lemon juice and Tabasco in my opinion.

"THERE AIN'T NO TREAT,
LIKE A BREADED MEAT,
AND I'LL BLOW
ANYONE
WOT FINDS ONE."

BY FILLET LARKIN

"THERE WAS A YOUNG AUSTRIAN COUNT,
WHO LUNCHED AN INORDINATE AMOUNT,
HE'D DINE WITH HIS PITBULL,
ORDER THOUSANDS OF SCHNITZEL,
AND EAT 'TIL THEY CARRIED HIM OUT."

BY SPIKE MILLIGRAM

A PERFECTLY ROASTED BIRD: CHICKEN/DUCK/ PHEASANT/PARTRIDGE/GUINEA FOWL

MY DEATH ROW MEAL WOULD BE ROAST CHICKEN, RICE AND COLESLAW WITH SOY SAUCE ON THE RICE, AND LOADS OF HOT SAUCE ON EVERYTHING. WHAT'S YOURS? THERE'S NO TURKEY IN THIS SECTION BECAUSE MY MUM ALWAYS DOES TWO DUCKS AT CHRISTMAS. THEY'RE LESS DRY AND CHEAPER THAN A RIP OFF MASSIVE TURKEY.

This isn't really a recipe, it's a guide to cooking birds as best you can:

— Never cook a bird straight from the fridge. Get it out at least an hour before cooking.

— Season immediately and season well. Both the skin and the cavity. You are cooking this bird whole, so it's impossible to season the breast by only seasoning the skin. Get inside the bird and get in there straight after taking it out of the fridge, then the seasoning has time to penetrate the meat.

— You want a really hot oven, full blast is best. 220°C–250°C.

— Cook your bird upside down for the first three quarters of the time you cook it. If you haven't got a wire rack to cook it on, chop onions or potatoes into think rounds and place them in the middle of the roasting try to make a platform for your bird.

— Rub the seasoned bird all over with some olive oil and lemon juice too if you fancy it (remember you've already salted it when you took it out the fridge). Now, put your bird, breast side down on its platform (or wire roasting rack) and bang it in the oven.

— The juices that would otherwise have seeped out of the breast and into the cavity, are now seeping into the breast. I promise you this will give you perfectly juicy fowl each and every time. Three quarters of the way through the time you are cooking it, turn the bird over however you can.

— Most people over cook birds. Chicken especially.

If you want to really cook it up, we'd be supportive of you removing the legs (and thighs) from the bird and cooking them separately (barring chicken, which should stay as it was made). We'd recommend confit-ing them particularly (which, if you persevere through this section, we will come to next). The legs will cook hunky dory in the following methods, but not as beautifully as if you confited them in olive oil, or even better, in duck or goose fat.

One of the benefits of getting meat in a butcher's over the supermarket, is that you can ask for stuff like the legs being removed. If you want to really get them going, get them to remove the wing tips and the wishbone too. The wing tips because they look horrible and the wishbone because carving will be easier later.

If you want to add flavourings to your bird, by all means do so, but don't overstuff the cavity (it changes the cooking time.) I like a few bay leaves, a couple of crushed garlic cloves still in their skin, maybe some thyme and half a lemon if I'm really going for it. And I never bother trussing the bird, in fact, take that bloody string off so you can get to the inside properly.

One final tip, as with all meat, is to rest it once it is cooked. With steak and things they say you should rest it as long as you cook it, but that'd be silly with a chicken. Put foil over it and rest it, upside down again, for at least 15 minutes before you hack it up. The juices will be visible and held in the meat which will be soft, tender and juicy.

What resting does do, is make skin go back from crispy to soft. For me this is no real bother as I'd choose juicy meat over crispy skin DAY AFTER DAY AFTER DAY. Roast chicken is about chicken. Not chicken skin.

Here are some cooking times for this method, to give you perfect birds based on them being an average size. If you've got a whopper on your hands, up the time by the percent you reckon it is bigger than normal – 30% bigger chicken than normal, 30% longer in the oven):

Chicken: Place upside-down in the oven for 45 minutes. Turn and roast the right way up for 15 minutes at the end to brown the skin.

Duck: Brown all over in a frying pan as best you can and then place upside-down in the oven for 20 minutes and then 10 minutes the right way up.

Pheasant: Brown all over in a frying pan as best you can and then cook breast-side down for 12 minutes and the right way up for the final 4 minutes.

Partridge: You fly mother funker! Brown all over in a frying pan as best you can and cook breast-side down for 8 minutes and then the right way up for the final 3 minutes.

Guinea fowl: Brown all over in a frying pan as best you can and then cook breast-side down for 30 minutes and then the right way up for the final 15 minutes.

How cooked duck and game birds are is less important than how cooked chicken is. Make sure the juices run clear when you skewer deeply into a meaty bit. But, don't forget that leg and thigh meat is naturally a bit pink when cooked, especially close to the bone. If the meat breaks into strands when you pull at it and comes away from the bone, you're in clover.

CONFIT FOWL

VARITIES IN TEXTURE AND FLAVOUR ARE KEY TO KEEPING YOUR SANDWICH GAME STRONG. IT'S NOT THE FIRST TIME WE'VE SAID THAT YOU CAN TREAT THE SAME INGREDIENT IN TWO DIFFERENT WAYS AND GET TWO DIFFERENT RESULTS.

IMAGINE YESTERDAY YOU TOOK THE LEGS OFF YOUR DUCK AND THEN ROASTED THE REST OF IT (PAGE 176). YOU COULD NOW, PEEL THE SKIN FROM THE LEGS AND PUT IT TO ONE SIDE TO TURN INTO SCRATCHINGS WHEN, AND IF, YOU CAN BE ARSED.

CONFIT MEANS COOKING SOMETHING VERY SLOWLY, IN A BATH OF FAT. AND THAT'S WHAT YOU'RE GOING TO DO TO THESE LEGS YOU'VE GOT. SAY THOSE WORDS AGAIN, "A BATH OF FAT." TO GET FLAVOUR INTO THE LEGS BEFORE YOU DO THIS, YOU NEED TO CURE THEM IN A SALT AND SUGAR MIX FOR 4-24 HOURS BEFORE COOKING.

---

4 duck legs

100g Salt

1 tsp ground black pepper

1 cinnamon stick (optional)

2 star anise (optional)

Leaves from three thyme stalks (optional)

2 bay leaves, dried or nicked from your neighbour's garden (optional)

250ml cheap olive oil (or 250g duck fat)

Find a spice grinder, blender or pestle and mortar. Add the salt, black pepper and any spices or herbs you think might taste good. Blitz. When the spices/herbs and salt have formed a powder coat each leg in a good layer rubbing it in everywhere, before laying them in a tray that isn't made of metal and covering with clingfilm . Leave in the fridge for 4-24 hours to cure.

When ready, preheat the oven to 150°C Wash the duck legs so that the majority of the salt is removed. Pat dry and lay in a relatively snug, oven safe bowl or little roasting dish. Cover completely with the oil (or duck fat) and make a cartouche to cover it all over. (p.158).

Place in the hot oven for 3 hours.

Remove from the oven and carefully remove the legs from the hot oil (or fat) and allow to cool. Tongs would be handy here if you have them? Or two forks maybe? Pick the meat from the bones. Reserve the oil/fat when cooked and store in the fridge until next time. This will keep for a good few months.

You can use the meat as it is. Try some. But, you could also pan-fry some of the picked meat in some oil or duck fat until it's all crispy and nice and then whack it in your sandwich?

This technique will work for the legs of any bird Even rabbit legs lend themselves well to this method. And partridge legs are an awesome snack if you do this then fry them brown in a pan!

PARFAIT

PARFAIT AND PÂTÉ ARE WONDERFUL THINGS IN A SANDWICH. WHO ARE WE KIDDING? THEY ARE WONDERFUL THINGS IN LIFE.

IN THE CONTEXT OF SANDWICHES, THINK OF PÂTÉ, AND ITS SMOOTH COUSIN PARFAIT, AS MEAT BUTTER. "MEAT BUTTER" – GOD LIFE IS SWEET. DO NOT FORGET TO TRY A LAYER OF PÂTÉ ON YOUR BREAD, NEXT TIME YOU MAKE A MEATY-LITTLE-TREAT OF A SANDWICH. AND HAVE A LOOK AT THE BÁNH MÌ RECIPE ON PAGE 86.

200g chicken or duck livers

200g unsalted butter

1 red onion, finely chopped

1 garlic clove, grated

1 tsp salt

1 tbsp sweet Sherry

½ tsp dried chilli flakes

½ tsp ground black pepper

Find your blender or food processor, you'll need it later.

Start by melting 50g of the unsalted butter in a frying pan over a medium heat. When it is frothing, add the onion and the garlic and half the salt. Sweat for 5–6 minutes until soft and just starting to caramelise.

At this point, add the booze to the pan and stand back as it may flame. This is not an issue – it's just the alcohol burning off. Don't panic, let it subside, which it will do, we promise.

Remove the cooked onions from the pan onto a plate and add another 50g of butter. When this is foaming, lay out the livers in the pan and cook for a full minute on each side until just browning. Add the remaining salt as well as the black pepper and chilli flakes. Toss the livers in the butter before taking off the heat.

Finally, blend the livers in the food processor with the onions and the remaining butter to a perfectly smooth paste and decant into nice little bowls to be eaten later with toast and chutney.

If you are going to use this straight away, go for it, smoosh it all over the place. However, if you want to keep it in the fridge, melt a little more butter in a pan and pour this over the top of the pâté in its containers. This will create an airtight seal, which will mean the pâté can keep for weeks.

RILLETTES

IF YOU'RE LUCKY AND IN FRANCE ON YOUR HOLIDAYS, YOU MIGHT COME ACROSS RILLETTES MADE WITH RABBIT, DUCK, CHICKEN OR GOOSE. ORDER IT. THIS HOWEVER, IS A RECIPE FOR THE MOST CLASSIC OLD FASHIONED ONE OF ALL. GOOD OLD PORK!

500g pork belly, skin removed, cut into 5cm cubes

½ tbsp Salt

1 garlic clove, peeled and halved

2 bay leaves

1 tsp whole black peppercorns

2 cloves

200ml white wine

Preheat the oven to 160°C.

Cut the pork belly into large cubes and toss them in a roasting tray with the salt, garlic, bay leaves, pepper and cloves. Put them in a single layer and add the wine. Cover with greaseproof paper and then two sheets of tin foil and place in the preheated oven for 3 hours.

Once your pork is ready, strain the liquid into a bowl, removing the bay leaves, pepper and cloves, and keep to one side. Meanwhile, start tearing at the pork with a couple of forks so that you create a pile of strands of pork belly.

Take half your reserved liquid and add this to the pile of pork. Massage with your hands so that the fat is absorbed into the meat. Taste a little and adjust the seasoning, if necessary. When you are happy, press the meat into a nice bowl or a terrine mould and pour over the remaining liquid and fat from the cooking. This will soak in and then cool on top and create an airtight seal. Keep in the fridge and use as and when you want to blow your mind.

In a sandwich made with toast and cornichons or a pickle of your choosing, this is one of the world's great treats. And brilliant for picnics.

BRAWN (AKA HEAD CHEESE)

IF YOU ARE A TINY BIT SQUEAMISH, DO NOT BOTHER WITH THIS RECIPE. IT IS LITERALLY THE PICKED AND SET FACE OF A PIG. IF, LIKE US, YOU ARE WILLING TO DO ALMOST ANYTHING IN THE SEARCH FOR INSANE FLAVOUR, THEN LOOK THAT LITTLE PIGGY STRAIGHT IN THE EYE AND ANNOUNCE THAT HEAD CHEESE IS TO BE MADE.

1 pig's head (4–5kg)

1 pig's trotter

2 large onions, halved

1 garlic bulb, halved

1 bunch of parsley, stalks and leaves separated

4 star anise

4 bay leaves

250ml white wine

You are going to need to prepare the face that stares up at you from your chopping board. Well done for getting to this point though.

Start by chopping off the ears. These can be singed with a flame (in the gas hob or under the grill. In a restaurant they'd blowtorch it) to remove any hairs, and should then be thoroughly washed to remove any burnt hair or wax, hehe.

Next you are going to need to trim off the eyelashes with scissors. No one wants an eyelash in their brawn. And finally, you're going to need to singe, then wash away, any facial hairs the hog might have. They are often shaved with disposable razors in restaurants.

Place it in a large pot with the ears, onions, garlic, parsley stalks, spices and wine, topping the pot up with water so that the face is completely submerged, then top with a cartouche (p.158).

Bring to the boil and skim off any scum that has risen to the surface by taking off the cartouche and spooning it out. Turn down the heat, cartouche back on and simmer ever so gently for 3–4 hours, until the meat is falling from the bones. Turn off the heat and leave to cool. When you can, put your hands in, take the head out and put it in something appropriately large. Strain the liquid, making sure to keep it and discarding the veg and things. Pick through the meat removing all bones and teeth and anything else inedible. Bear in mind all the fat and skin is edible. Do not throw it away.

Slices the ears as finely as you can all the way across their width and mix them up thoroughly with the meat you have and half its volume in fat. Press the lot into a terrine mould or something similar. If you so wish you could keep one ear's worth of slices and treat it like the pork scratchings (p.173). Finally, pour enough of the cooking liquid into the container as it needs to cover the meat. Knock the mould a few times with your wooden spoon to help the liquid find its way down through the meat. Once it seems to have soaked in, pick up the terrine or whatever you're making the brawn in and drop it (firmly but not aggressively from about three inches off the work surface). This knocks out air and helps get the liquid everywhere. Top up and repeat as necessary until liquid is sitting, in a small quantity on top of the brawn. With it well and truly covered, wrap the whole lot in clingfilm and place in the fridge for 6 hours until the brawn is completely set.

You can treat it in two ways now. Either slice it and place in a sandwich with some nice tart pickles, or breadcrumb a slice (p.219) and deep fry it, place that in a sandwich with some pickles and hot sauce and sit back and look as smug as a dog that has just realised it can lick its own balls. Keep the brawn in its terrine container in the fridge and remove it slice by slice whenever you want some.

If you wanted to be really jazzy you could line the terrine mould first with clingfilm, leaving loads extra on all sides and once it has set you can turn it out onto a COLD plate and keep it in the fridge. The jelly will melt on a warm plate and the whole thing will slide around like an ice cube, fall from the tray and take out fido during his heinous act.

"GOD SAVE OUR GRACIOUS QUEEN,
CHICKEN BREAST IS TOO LEAN,
GOD SAVE THE QUEEN.
MAYO'S VICTOROUS,
CURRY POWDER'S GLORIOUS,
FOODIES ABHOR-OR US,
GOD SAVE THE QUEEN."

BY HRH PRINCE FILLET

CORONATION CHICKEN

IT'S WHAT SHE WOULD HAVE WANTED.

500g chicken thighs, skin, bone and shifty looking bits removed

150ml Greek yoghurt

½ bunch of coriander, stalks finely chopped, leaves picked and roughly chopped

1 tsp ground cinnamon

5 grinds of your pepper grinder

A pinch of saffron

1 tsp salt

Index finger sized piece of ginger, peeled and grated

2 tbsps curry powder

150ml mayonnaise

50g mango chutney

50g sultanas
(feel free to not use these. My Dad hates sultanas)

Preheat the oven to 200°C. Chop you thigh meat chunkily and place it in a mixing bowl. Add a third of your yoghurt, the chopped coriander stalks, the cinnamon, pepper, saffron, salt, grated ginger and half the curry powder to the bowl and mix well. Leave to marinade for 30 minutes.

Lay the chicken out on a greaseproof-lined baking tray and roast in the hot oven for 10ish minutes until the meat is just cooked through. Remove from the oven and allow to cool.

Meanwhile, combine the mayonnaise, remaining yoghurt, remaining curry powder, the mango chutney and sultanas in a bowl. Add the cooked chicken thigh pieces and mix well to coat and combine. Stir through the chopped coriander leaves and you are good to go.

I'd be tempted to have this completely on its own in a sandwich. Maybe butter the bread…

FISH

FRIED SARDINES

IF YOU HAVE EVER BEEN TO ISTANBUL OR THE FUN END OF THE GOLBORNE ROAD, YOU WILL UNDERSTAND THAT A FRIED SARDINE IN A SANDWICH IS A VERY SPECIAL THING. THE RICH, OILY FLESH OF THE FISH, A LIGHTLY SPICED DUSTING OF FLOUR, A GOOD FRYING FOR SOME CRUNCH... IT IS TOO MUCH, TOO GOOD.

4 filleted sardines, don't try and do this yourself

75g plain flour

Zest of 1 lemon

1 tsp paprika

1 tsp Salt

75ml rapeseed oil

In a mixing bowl, combine the flour, lemon zest, paprika and salt. Mix well with your hands before dredging the sardines in the mixture. Shake off the excess.

Get your oil hot in a large frying pan. Lay the sardines in the oil carefully so as not to splash hot oil on your hands, and fry for 1 minute on each side. You want a nice crispy layer to form. When cooked, lay on some paper towel and sprinkle with a tiny amount of salt and a little extra paprika.

These will be a delight in any sandwich with a tart sauce or mayonnaise and some pickled vegetables or chillies.

FRIED MUSSELS

WHY THE TURKS ARE SO DRAWN TO FRYING FISH AND THEN PLACING IT INSIDE SANDWICHES WE WILL NEVER KNOW, BUT THANK MOSES THEY ARE AS THIS IS ONE OF THE BESTEST POSSIBLE THINGS IN THE WHOLE WORLD.

1kg mussels, washed and debearded, open ones discarded

75g plain flour

25g cornflour

1 tsp salt

¼ tsp chilli powder

150ml sparkling water, ice cold

1 tsp sumac

1 litre rapeseed oil

You need to start by opening the mussels, which is a remarkably simple enterprise. Take a heavy-bottomed, lidded saucepan, large enough to fit the mussels inside, and place over a high heat. When a splash of water whistles and fizzes in the pan, tip the cleaned mussels into the pot and place a snug-fitting lid on top. Allow to steam for 2 minutes before shaking the pan vigorously. Give them another 30 seconds and then turn them out into a colander. Allow to cool for a minute before going through and picking the mussel out of each shell, using an empty shell as a pair of pincers.

Place the flour, cornflour, chilli powder and salt in a bowl and slowly add your very cold sparkling water, whisking vigorously as you go. You want a batter the consistency of single cream, that coats a finger when dunked in it, but leaves the knuckle visible.

Place the oil in a high-sided pan and warm it over a medium flame. If you have a thermometer, use it and monitor the oil until it reaches 180°C or until a piece of bread dropped inside browns within 20 seconds.

Now the good bit. Dump the mussels into the batter and drop them carefully into the hot oil one by one. They will take no more than a minute to become perfectly golden brown and crispy. Remove them to some paper towel with a slotted spoon or something and sprinkle with a little more salt and the sumac. The sumac's sourness does the same thing as lemon juice, but won't make your crunchy batter go soft.

Once your fried mussels have cooled off a little, sample a few for your own pleasure, and then place a good pile of them in a sandwich that contains a sharp sauce, like lemon mayo maybe?!

FRIED SQUID

I MEAN, COME ON, WHAT SORT OF ENTICEMENT DO YOU REALLY NEED? COOK THIS FAST, AND AT A HIGH HEAT. THERE WILL BE NO CHEWY-CHEWY-RUBBER-JOHNNY FOR YOU, MY FRIEND.

500g squid, a nice big one, and its tentacles, cleaned by the fishmonger and left whole

1 tbsp plain flour

1 tbsp cornflour

100ml sparkling water, ice cold

Salt

2 litres rapeseed oil

For the Morunos sauce:

1 tsp cumin powder

1 tsp coriander powder

1 tsp sweet smoked paprika

2 tbsps lemon juice

4 tbps olive oil

Salt

Take a knife and run it up the inside of the squid's body, opening it up and allowing you to lay it flat on your board. Use the tip of the knife and gently score the inside of the squid with a criss-cross, chequerboard pattern all over it's body. This will allow it to grab hold of your batter. Cut the squid into strips, squares, rhombuses, who cares, but make sure they are a good consistent size.

In a mixing bowl, combine the flour, cornflour and salt before slowly adding the sparkling water whilst frantically whisking all the while. When you have a nice batter the consistency of single cream, stop, and drop your prepped squid in.

Fill a high-sided pan with the rapeseed oil and placing over a medium flame to come up to temperature. If you have a thermometer, use it and monitor the oil until it reaches 180°C or until a piece of bread dropped inside browns within 20 seconds.

Now drop ⅓ of the little squiddy pieces into the hot oil and cook for 2 minutes. Move them around immediately and regularly with a slotted spoon to keep them from sticking to one another. Remove to a plate with some paper towel on it, sprinkle with salt and repeat with the remaining squid.

Whisk up the ingredients for the Morunos sauce, drizzle it all over the squid and stick it in a baguette to recreate Madrid's great sandwich, the bocadillo de calamares.

CONFIT TUNA

NO ONE WOULD BAT AN EYELID, LET ALONE PASS BLAME, IF YOU FLIPPED ON PAST THIS RECIPE AND FLICKED US TWO FINGERS BEFORE HEADING TO YOUR LOCAL SUPERMARKET TO BUY TINNED TUNA IN BULK. BUT, IF YOU ARE EVEN REMOTELY INTRIGUED BY THIS RECIPE, PLEASE GIVE IT A GO – YOU WILL NOT REGRET IT. THIS IS ONE OF THE SIMPLEST WAYS TO COOK TUNA, AND IT WILL GIVE YOU AN INGREDIENT THAT IS AS STAND-OUT IN YOUR SANDWICH AS IT IS IN A SALAD, OR AS PART OF A BILLY-BIG-BOLLOCKS GOURMET SPREAD.

1kg tuna loin (please buy the best, high-welfare tuna you can afford, this is special, so speak to that fishmonger you're always going on about)

1 tbsp salt

2 tsps dried chilli flakes

1 tsp fennel seeds

2 tsps caster sugar

500ml extra virgin olive oil

Zest of 2 lemons

2 garlic cloves, whole

1 small bunch of parsley

You are going to need to salt the tuna for a few hours to firm it up before you confit it. Blitz or pestle and mortar the salt, chilli flakes, fennel seeds and sugar to a fine dust. Cut the tuna into nice big chunks (you should get about 4 even pieces), and cover in the salt mix. Place in a container in the fridge and leave for at least 4 hours. You could do this overnight if it makes more sense for you logistically.

When ready, preheat the oven to 100°C. Take the tuna chunks out of the fridge and wash off any excess cure. Pat them dry and place them in a roasting tray just large enough to fit them in a single layer. Cover them completely with the olive oil and add the lemon zest, garlic and parsley, pressing it all under the oil and placing a cartouche on top (p.158).

Place the tray uncovered apart from the cartouche, in the oven for 1 hour. Remove and allow to cool. You can keep the tuna under the oil for a month at least in the fridge. When you are ready to use it, simply remove a chunk, flake it with your fingers and use it in a sandwich. This is outrageously good with Salsa Romesco (see p.134) and bitter salad leaves or with mayonnaise and lemon juice, but we will leave it up to you.

BRANDADE

THIS SUPER SOFT AND THREATENINGLY RICH DISH OF WHIPPED SALT COD IS ONE OF THE BEST THINGS IN THE WORLD. YOU COULD, AND PERHAPS SHOULD, USE IT AS A BASE FOR EVERY SANDWICH YOU EVER MAKE, EVER. DOUBLE DARE YOU TO MAKE A SANDWICH WITH BRANDADE, FRIED SQUID (PAGE 190) AND SOFT-BOILED EGGS AND LOADS OF PARSLEY AND LEMON JUICE.

250g salt cod, soaked in water for 24 hours in the fridge, in as many changes of water as you can bothered to do.

250ml full fat milk

2 bay leaves

1 clove

5 black peppercorns

½ onion, in one piece, with the clove stuck in it

250g floury potatoes, peeled and cut up into small cube-ish pieces

2 garlic cloves, peeled but left whole

100ml extra virgin olive oil

Please do not skip the soaking of the salt cod. If you do, you will end up with something offensively salty and we will never speak to you again. We would recommend changing the soaking water every 6 hours or so.

Take your cod from the soaking water and pop it in a saucepan with the milk, bay leaves, peppercorns, clove and onion. Bring this to the boil over a high heat, reduce to a simmer and cook for 3 minutes before removing the cod and keeping it to one side while you cook the potatoes.

Now, remove the onion and add the potatoes and garlic to the milk. Bring to the boil again and simmer for 8–10 minutes until the potatoes are well and truly cooked. Pluck out the bay leaves, peppercorns and the onion and clove, but leave the potatoes and garlic inside the milk.

In a food processor, add the milk, soft potatoes, garlic and the salt cod and pulse 10 or so times so that you have a rough paste. Add the olive oil and pulse again to get the whole thing to come together. Don't whizz it for ages into too smooth a texture, as this will leave you with a gluey finish. Pulsing will bring the brandade together and leave you with a light, rich texture – you just have to accept a few minor lumps and bumps.

Check your seasoning (the salt cod should have done all the work that adding salt would normally do) and start slathering this on everything.

This vintage Tabasco pepper
sauce has been especially
bottled to become the
private stock of

Max's Sandwich Shop

Presented with due ceremony
in the best tradition of the
McIlhenny Company.

President/CEO

PRAWN MAYONNAISE

WHAT COULD BE A MORE NECESSARY WEAPON IN YOUR SANDWICH ARMOURY THAN A FAILSAFE PRAWN MAYONNAISE RECIPE? WE'RE NOT TRYING TO BE CLEVER WITH THIS ONE. PRAWNS, MAYO, AND NOT MUCH ELSE. BUT, IN BETWEEN SOME SOFT WHITE BREAD WITH THE CRUNCH OF SHREDDED GEM LETTUCE, WELL, HEAVEN IS A PLACE ON EARTH.

150g cooked and
peeled prawns

1 tbsp mayonnaise (buy
Hellmann's or see p.122)

5 drops of Tabasco sauce

5 drops of Worcestershire
sauce

A small pinch of salt

1 big grind of black pepper

Juice of ¼ lemon

1 baby gem lettuce,
shredded

Find a bowl, any bowl, and combine all the ingredients save the lettuce. Mix well and taste with your little finger. Adjust the salt, acid and heat according to your own personal preference.

Find some soft, fresh bread, butter said bread, cover with as much prawn mayonnaise as is polite, top with shredded lettuce, close the sandwich and beam with delight.

Occasionally I don't listen to my own advice and have this in a hollowed out mini baguette and sometimes I put avocado in there too. And crushed up crispy bacon would be pretty mega too.

FISH FINGERS

HOW HARD CAN IT BE, RIGHT? NOT HARD AT ALL. SO GIVE THAT OLD PERVERT CAPTAIN BIRDSEYE THE FINGER AND MAKE THE BEST FISH FINGERS IN THE WORLD.

150g nice white fish, boned and skinned (cod is back in vogue, but who knows? Haddock? Whiting and sole would be delicious…)

1 litre rapeseed oil

2 medium eggs, beaten

100g plain flour

2 tsps salt

1 tsp ground black pepper

150g breadcrumbs
(See Ned Halley's Breadcrumbs on p. 218, or buy some panko, or ask the baker if they've got some you can buy)

1 litre rapeseed oil

Lay out three containers or bowls and place the beaten eggs in one, the flour, salt and pepper in another, and the breadcrumbs in the final one. Cut the white fish into decent sized fingers about the size of a Mars Bar.

Drop the fish pieces into the flour, covering well and shaking off any excess. Then put them in the egg, ensuring they are completely coated and finally, into the breadcrumbs. Place the finished fish finger on a plate while you complete the set.

Place the oil in a high-sided pan and warm it over a medium flame. If you have a thermometer, use it and monitor the oil until it reaches 180°C or until a piece of bread dropped inside browns within 10 seconds.

When ready, carefully lower the fish fingers into the hot oil and allow to cook for 2 minutes before removing and draining on some paper towel. Do this in batches.

Once all the fish fingers are fried, you are good to go. Layer them up in a sandwich and douse with mayonnaise, preferably mayonnaise with sharpness and tang – malt vinegar mayo, lemon mayo and sweet herb mayo would all be perfect (all p.124).

Now I think about it, whack some gherkins in there too. And shred some iceberg lettuce. AND USE BUTTER!!! And don't be shy about putting hot sauce in.

KIPPER PÂTÉ

I HAVE MADE A NUMBER OF LITTLE FILMS FOR A COMPANY CALLED *VICE*. IN ONE CALLED MAX'S FISH SANDWICH I MADE KIPPER PÂTÉ TO GO WITH LAMB. SO WE THOUGHT WE'D BETTER GIVE YOU THE RECIPE.

200g kipper fillets (it's perfectly good with the unpeppered smoked mackerel fillets available in all the supermarkets too)

1 tbsp crème fraîche

1 tbsp malt vinegar

2½ cm piece of peeled, fresh horseradish, grated (or 1 big tbsp horseradish sauce)

½ tsp Salt

6 grinds of black pepper

Find a blender or food processor. Pile in all the ingredients and pulse 8–10 times. That's it. Smear it in a sandwich, smear it on toast – smear it on the floor and ceiling for all we care. Whatever you do, have it with a pickle or two. And washed down with a glass of wine. Or two.

It'll keep in the fridge for a week.

VEG

DEEP FRIED BROCCOLI

250g broccoli, florets broken into little pieces, stalks cut into batons

2 litres rapeseed oil

2 tbsps gram (chickpea) flour

1 tsp Salt

4 tbsps ice cold sparkling water

Make a batter by frantically whisking together the flour, salt and sparkling water. You want it to coat your finger so that you can still see the detail of your knuckle. Sounds mental, but try it – it works a dream each time. Too thick? More water. Too thin? More gram flour.

Heat the oil in a high-sided saucepan until it is 180°C or until a flick of batter sizzles satisfyingly in the oil.

When your batter is ready, add the broccoli to the batter and mix well. Pick up a piece at a time and allow all but a thin film of batter to drip off. Fry the florets, for two minutes, in batches of 5 or 6 so you don't overcrowd the pan. Pop them on some paper towel and sprinkle with a touch more salt. Repeat until all your broccoli is fried.

Boff in a sandwich with leftover curry or dunk on its own into lemon mayonnaise (p.124)

CHARRED GREENS

BURNT GREENS, PARTICULARLY BURNT BRASSICAS, ARE DELICIOUS. SO DELICIOUS THAT YOU MIGHT STRUGGLE TO EAT AN UNBURNT BRASSICA EVER AGAIN. TRY THIS OUT IT COULDN'T BE SIMPLER. BURNT GREENS LIKE THIS LOVE PINE NUT TARATOR (PAGE 141) BETTER THAN ANYTHING ELSE.

250g greens, preferably something hearty like hispi cabbage, broccoli, stalky kale or cavolo nero

1 tsp Maldon sea salt

1 tsp dried chilli flakes

1 tbsp extra virgin olive oil

Juice of ½ lemon

Preheat the oven to 250°C

Cut your greens into nice big chunks. Cabbage can be quartered or cut into eighths, depending on its size. Broccoli can be treated the same, but tender stem or purple sprouting are best left as they are.

Place the your greens in a roasting tray and toss with the salt, dried chilli flakes and olive oil. Press into a single layer and place in the oven. Roast hard for 15 minutes before removing and turning the veg. Return to the oven and roast hard for another 15 mins. There you are. Soft and succulent greens with delicious burnt edges. Hit immediately with the lemon juice and then leave to cool slightly before eating or boffing in a sarnie.

CROQUETAS

THERE IS NO ONE ON THIS PLANET WHO HAS EVER SAID THEY DISLIKE CROQUETAS. THAT IS THAT. AND IF YOU WANT TO BE POPULAR AND HAVE A GUARANTEED WINNER IN YOUR ARMOURY, YOU SHOULD LEARN TO MAKE THESE.

BELOW THERE IS A (HOPEFULLY) SIMPLE AND (HOPEFULLY) FOOLPROOF RECIPE FOR A PLAIN CROQUETA. MAKE IT, ENJOY IT, BANG IT IN A SANDWICH. THEN, NEXT TIME YOU HAVE COLD MEAT, SOME HAM, SOME ROAST CHICKEN, SOME PRAWNS, CAULIFLOWER, PEAS OR THE ENDS OF A PUNGENT TALEGGIO OR MATURE CHEDDAR, MAKE IT SMALL BY CHOPPING OR GRATING IT AND ADD IT TO THIS RECIPE.

150g butter

1 white onion, finely diced

¼ tsp Salt

200g plain flour

1 litre full fat milk

10 grinds of black pepper

2 litres rapeseed oil

Place your heaviest bottomed saucepan over a medium heat. Add the butter to the pan and allow to melt and froth. Add the onion and reduce the heat to low, add the salt and sweat away for 10–12 minutes until the onions are soft and not coloured.

Add the flour and cook out for 2 minutes in the buttery onions. Next add an introductory splash of milk and stir this excitedly into the floury-buttery-onions. Add a splash more milk and repeat. At this point you should probably be using a nice firm whisk. A splash more milk, repeat.

Now glug in the remaining milk and stir until you have a smooth and thickening sauce. Allow to bubble away gently for 5 minutes, stirring occasionally, until you have a nice, thick béchamel. It is at this juncture that you can add your choice of filling (peas/prawns /ham/cauliflower/nutmeg/cheese/etc.). Decant into a tray or container, lined with greaseproof paper and smear roughly flat with your wooden spoon or anything really, and chill in the fridge until set which will take at least two hours.

Once set, remove from the fridge and prepare your crumbing section. One container with the whisked eggs, one with the 2 tablespoons of flour, and one with the breadcrumbs.

Put a few tablespoons in a cup of boiling water. Use them to make quenelles (posh little rugby balls) of the béchamel. Watch a video online of how to do this properly rather than me trying to explain. Drop the quenelles into the flour.

For the crumb:

5 tbsps plain flour

150g dried white
breadcrumbs like Ned
Halley would make
p.218 (you want either
really really stale bread
blitzed up, or buy panko
breadcrumbs, or ask
the baker if they do
breadcrumbs)

3 medium eggs, whisked up,
on a plate

Roll 'em about and then send them into the egg and then the breadcrumbs, ensuring that you get a good even coating on your croqueta. When you have done them all, turn your attention to frying.

Heat the rapeseed oil in a high-sided pan over a medium flame to 190°C. If you have a thermometer, use it and monitor the oil; alternatively, place a cube of stale bread in the pan and when it fizzes and goes brown within 20 seconds you are probably at peak oil temperature for frying.

Fry in batches of 6–8 for 2–3 minutes.

Remove and drain on paper towel while you complete frying the rest of the croquetas. Once you have them all fried, eat one or two, and pop the rest in a sandwich for you and your friends. As a general rule, pick one of our sauces, pick some nice crunchy salad leaves and/or some fresh herbs, add something pickled, and make it into a sandwich. Just look at The Spaniard on p.28. You will have never been more contented. End of.

"THERE WAS A YOUNG MAN FROM UPTOWN,
POOR ENDOWMENT HAD LEFT HiM QUITE DOWN.
HiS ONLY WAY OF SURViVAL,
THE ONLY SURE FiRE REViVAL,
WAS TWO EGGS, RED SAUCE AND HASH BROWNS"

BY SPiKE MiLLiGRAM

HASH BROWNS

2 large potatoes,
King Edward or
Roosevelt preferably

½ white onion

1 tsp salt

Plenty of ground
black pepper

1 egg

2 tbsps plain flour

Hash browns can be many shapes and sizes. The important thing is to have hash browns. This one is crispy and moist.

Find a bowl and fill it with cold water. Find a grater and locate the coarse side. Don't worry about peeling your spuds, just grate the hell out of them straight into the water. Now leave them. Thirty minutes should do you.

Grate your onion on the same side as your potato, and place in a bowl of its own. Add the salt, plenty of pepper, the cracked egg and the flour. Fork it about a bit and leave it.

Return to your soaking grated potato. Do not drain it. Lay a tea towel in a sieve, or colander, in another bowl. Lift out the soaked strands of potato and place them in the towel. Over the soaking bowl, bring up the four corners of the cloth and twist until it is a VERY tight ball. Squeeze like a demon.

Milky liquid will leave the potato and mix with the soaking water. If you twist it, it will squeeze tighter and tighter. After a minute or two of hardcore squeezing, the potato will be pretty much dry.

Empty it into the bowl with everything else and mix with your hands. Carefully pour the water out of the potato bowl making sure to leave behind any white residue sitting at the bottom. This is starch (God's glue) and it is good for your hash brown. Once you have just that left at the bottom of your bowl, add it to the hash brown mix, and mix.

Place a frying pan over a medium heat. Warm a tablespoon of oil in the pan and drop tablespoons full of hash brown mix into the pan. Use the back of the spoon to flatten them a little. Cook for 2 minutes on the one side, turn, and then 2 minutes on the other. They should be brown and crunchy. If not, cook more. Remove from the pan and cook the rest. You could eat these alongside any egg-based breakfast, but add them to a sandwich and you're guaranteed a spot in Valhalla. Unexpectedly, these are a great addition to an ice cream sandwich.

PICKLED VEG SPRING ROLLS

We use a classic, quick pickling liquor by bringing to the boil (then cooling):

500ml white wine vinegar

250ml water

250g caster sugar

For the veg:

500g beansprouts

1 cucumber, sliced as thinly as possible, including skin and seeds

2 decent-sized red chillies, thinly sliced on the diagonal seeds and all

3 peeled and grated carrots

Spring roll wrappers

Put all the ingredients into the cold pickling liquor in a plastic container, cover with a cartouche (see p.158), pop a lid on and keep in the fridge for at least a day before making your spring rolls.

It will take a very long time to write down here how to roll up a spring roll. Do what I did, go online and watch a video. It's much easier than I thought it would be. Then fry them to your heart's content. You can buy the wrappers in a Chinese supermarket or online. Get the bigger ones.

CLAUDIA'S GUACAMOLE

OH CLAUDIA! WHAT A LEGEND YOU ARE. THIS MAKES ENOUGH FOR TWO PEOPLE EASILY.

2 tomatoes

2 avocados, stoned, peeled and chopped

½ red onion, grated coarsely

2 garlic cloves, finely grated and smooshed with salt into a purée

½ bunch of coriander, leaves and stalks finely chopped

1 tbsp sliced, pickled jalapeños, finely chopped

A massive pinch of salt

A smaller pinch of sugar

Juice of 1 lemon

Make a cross (two inch long cuts) with a knife not too deep in the bottom of the tomatoes. Throw them into a pan of boiling water. After a minute or two the skin will begin to peel back. At this point pour the boiling water down the sink and run the cold tap over the tomatoes until they're touchable. Peel off the skins and throw them away. Cut the tomatoes in half and remove the seeds with a teaspoon, chop out the hard little core and cut the tomatoes into tiny little pieces. Chuck in a big bowl.

Add the avocado and all the other ingredients. Mash it all up with a potato masher or the end of a whisk so that everything's got to know each other but isn't too smooth.

The secret to guacamole is the seasoning! If you try it and it isn't the most delicious thing ever, add some more acid (white wine vinegar or lemon juice) and more salt until it's perfect. Have it on toast or with fried eggs and crisps in a sandwich as we do at The Sandwich Shop! (p.44).

BEN'S COLESLAW

THIS IS VERY DIFFERENT TO THE RUNNIER, MORE CLASSIC MAYO-BASED SLAW OVER TO THE RIGHT.

USE THE FRESHEST, MOST DELICIOUS, SEASONAL VEG FOR THIS AND YOU'LL BE ROLLING IN THE HAY. IF IT IS SUMMER, FRESH RADISHES, COURGETTE , HISPI CABBAGE AND SWEETCORN COULD ALL BE PUT TO GOOD USE; IF IT'S WINTER, THEN RED CABBAGE, FENNEL, APPLES, BRUSSELS SPROUTS AND KALE ARE SOME OF THE FINEST COLESLAW MAKERS THERE ARE.

1kg good crunchy veg (cabbage is a great staple; otherwise, think of things that are delicious, seasonal and colourful)

½ tsp salt

2 tbsps white wine vinegar

2 tbsps extra virgin olive oil

2 tbsps Greek yoghurt

Juice of 1 lemon

First, cut up all your vegetables as thinly as you can. If you have a sharp knife and a steady hand, off you go. If you own a swish food processor with a slicing attachment, get it out. If you have a coarse grater, that'll probably be useful here too.

Place all the veg in a large mixing bowl, add the rest of the ingredients and mix well with your hands. You can scrunch and massage a little here, but not so much that you break down all the delicious crunch of your veg. Just enough that the flavours are all mingling and tingling.

Taste and adjust the seasoning. This is best made a little in advance so that the salt, vinegar and yoghurt have time to do their work and break everything down a little.

POMEGRANATE & PARSLEY SLAW

OH MY LORD THIS IS GOOD. ALL THE JOYS OF REGULAR COLESLAW, PLUS SOME DELICIOUS EXTRAS. THIS IS MUCH WETTER AND SLOPPIER THAN THE OTHER COLESLAW RECIPE WE'VE GIVEN YOU. TRY BOTH AND CHOOSE A FAVOURITE.

½ white cabbage, cut in half, core removed and sliced as thinly as possible

3 carrots, peeled and coarsely grated

1 onion, grated on the coarse side of the grater

1 bunch of parsley, stalks finely sliced, leaves left whole

1 pomegranate, seeds removed

A massive pinch of salt

For the dressing:

8 tbsps mayo
(and maybe more)

A massive squeeze of pomegranate molasses
(3–4 tbsps worth at least)

Juice of 1 lemon

Salt and pepper

Mix all the veg, (including the parsley stalks but not the leaves and pomegranate seeds) together in a large bowl, sprinkle with the salt and toss about. You want it all to start to soften a bit and break down. While all that gets to know itself, mix the dressing ingredients in a bowl.

Slather all over the veg, stirring and tossing all the while. It should be sloppy. If not, add more mayo. Leave it for half an hour and it'll get sloppier, and better.

You might need to add more salt, more acid and maybe even some sugar. Taste it and decide for yourself. Just before you eat it, put the pomegranate seeds and parsley in so they're fresh as daisies.

CRISPS
& CRUNCHY BITS

Nearly every sandwich needs crunch and salt. Crisps are a sneaky way of killing two birds with one stone. If you can't be bothered to make any of the items in this section, do yourself a favour and buy a bag of crisps that roughly correspond to the effect you are trying to achieve.

8 CRISPS AND HOW TO SANDWICH WITH THEM

SCAMPI FRIES

Firm friends with all your fishy bidness.

WALKERS

Flavour: Ready Salted.
Don't fancy making shoestring fries?

MCCOY'S

Flavour: Flaming Grilled Steak
Can't find cassava?

BRANNIGANS

Flavour: Roast Beef and Mustard.
In a ham sandwich... Oh my god.

DISCOS

Flavour: Salt and Vinegar
D. I. S. C. O give it a go.

DORITOS

Flavour: Cool Original.
MSG flavour crisps? Go on you devil.

MONSTER MUNCH

Flavour: Flaming Hot
Probably crap in a sandwich,
but what a crisp!

PORK SCRATCHINGS

Crush 'em up and whack 'em in.
A joy in so many sarnies.

SHOESTRING FRIES

200g potatoes like Maris Pipers or something, waxy ones fall apart less

2 litres rapeseed oil

Find yourself three things. A container or large bowl, a source of running water, and a sharp knife or Japanese mandolin.

Slice or mandolin each potato into the smallest and neatest little matchsticks you can achieve. You do not want these to be any thicker than 2 or 3mm . Submerge your little sticks of potatoes in ice-cold water and agitate with your hands for a minute.

Leave to soak for at least 10 minutes before moving into a colander or sieve to drain and dry out a bit. You want them to be in here drying for at least half an hour. Water and hot oil are not friends.

After half an hour heat the rapeseed oil in a high-sided pan over a medium flame to 190°C. If you have a thermometer, use it and monitor the oil; alternatively, place a cube of stale bread in the pan and when it is fizzing and brown you are probably at peak oil temperature for frying.

Drop the potato sticks into the hot oil in small batches and fry until they become golden brown shoestring fries. Place on some paper towel and season with a little salt. Repeat until you have a pile of perfectly crisp matchsticks.

Unsalted, these are The Sandwich Shop's most faithful crisp. Providing crunch to our wonderful Ham, Egg 'n' Chips since day one baby.

SWEET POTATO SHOESTRING FRIES

Just like normal potato shoestrings but unsurprisingly, much sweeter. A little less crunchy than potato ones too perhaps, but still wonderful. And these ones have got to be peeled. When they soak up juice in a sandwich they go a tiny bit chewy in a really nice way. They are so, so good with game and confit meats. We used them in Chris' Infamous Robocoq (p.105).

SWEET POTATO FRIES

2 large sweet potatoes, peeled

1 tsp Maldon sea salt

½ tsp sweet smoked paprika

1 rosemary sprig, leaves picked and finely chopped

2 tbsps rapeseed oil

Preheat the oven to 200°C.

Cut the sweet potatoes in half lengthways and then into as many thin wedges as you can (also lengthways).

Toss the wedges, salt, paprika, chopped rosemary and oil together so that the wedges are well coated.

Lay out the fries in a baking tray large enough to accommodate them in a single layer and place in the hot oven. Cook for 15–20 minutes until the fries are crisped and crisped and looking lovely.. Allow to cool before you use them in a sandwich – this will also allow them to crisp a little more as they cool.

VEGETABLE CRISPS

2 parsnips

2 beetroot

2 carrots

2 litres rapeseed oil

1 tsp Maldon sea salt

Dig out that Japanese mandolin again. Apart from the blood, it has been well worth the investment at this juncture, wouldn't you say?

Thinly slice each of the washed, but unpeeled, raw vegetables into 1mm thick rounds. Don't have a mandolin? Slice them with a vegetable peeler.

Heat the rapeseed oil in a high-sided pan over a medium flame to 190°C. If you have a thermometer, use it and monitor the oil; alternatively, place a cube of stale bread in the pan and when it is fizzing and brown you are probably at peak oil temperature for frying.

Fry the sliced vegetables in batches for 1 minute a time. Repeat until all the vegetables are fried. When fried, place in a shallow bowl lined with paper towel and season with some of the salt. That's it – couldn't be simpler.

These are a banger in a sanger or just in a bowl with 8 beers.

NED HALLEY'S BREADCRUMBS

Slice whatever old bread you have (fresh would be fine too). Cut those slices into soldiers. Put these on a baking tray in an oven at 120°C until they're completely dried out (at least an hour). Once they've gone cold, break them all up a bit, whack them in your food processor and blitz into breadcrumbs.

My Dad, who taught me all the world's breadcrumb secrets, lets them cool, puts them in a bag and beats them with a rolling pin to the desired texture.

FRIED BREADCRUMBS
OR MIGAS, IF YOU'RE SPANISH

200g bread, a few days old is perfect

4 garlic cloves, peeled but left whole

75ml extra virgin olive oil

½ tsp sweet smoked paprika

½ tsp Maldon sea salt

Start by blitzing the bread in a food processor to a coarse, fine gravel-like texture.

Set the heaviest bottomed frying pan you've got over a medium heat. Warm the olive oil in the pan and add the garlic cloves to flavour the oil. When they have sizzled a little and turned brown, remove the cloves and add the breadcrumbs to the pan.

Help the crumbs settle in an even layer with the back of a wooden spoon. I'm afraid that this is a recipe that needs a little attention from here on in. Leave the crumbs for 10 seconds or so and then turn them over with the spoon, leave again for 10 seconds and turn again. Continue like this until the crumbs are a caramel brown colour. When you are happy, remove from the heat and stir in the paprika and the salt. Mix well and then tip into a little bowl lined with paper towel to drain a little of the oil.

Use these to sprinkle on anything soft, that needs a bit of crunch.

CRISPY SEAWEED

A LITTLE KNOWN, AND SIMULTANEOUSLY OFT KNOWN FACT: CHINESE TAKEAWAY CRISPY SEAWEED IS IN FACT KALE. SO, AT LAST, YOU HAVE A USE FOR THAT KALE YOU KEEP BUYING AND LETTING GO MANKY AND PONDY IN THE BOTTOM OF THE FRIDGE. AND PLEASE, TREAT YOURSELF TO A NEW BAG BEFORE YOU MAKE THIS.

ALTERNATIVELY, IF YOU CAN'T BE ARSED TO HEAT THE OIL ETC., JUST POP IN TO YOUR LOCAL CHINESE TAKEAWAY AND BUY SOME ON YOUR WAY BACK FROM WORK. IT IS KALE AFTER ALL, AND THOSE GUYS HAVE MSG, WHICH IS DELICIOUS.

200g kale, stalks and leaves finely shredded

1 litre rapeseed oil

1 tsp Maldon sea salt

Find a large, high-sided saucepan. Add the oil and bring to about 180°C over a high flame. If you do not have a suitable thermometer, it's hot enough when a piece of kale added to the oil fizzes gently. Reduce the flame to low and add the kale a couple of handfuls at a time.

You want to fry in batches (do not overcrowd the pan as the kale will not fry so nicely). Each batch will only take about 30 seconds to become crispy. Remove with tongs or a slotted spoon and drain on paper towels. Season with salt while still warm. Fry all your kale in this manner. Don't worry if it doesn't seem that crunchy, cooling does wonders.

You can add other flavours to your finished crispy kale. Chilli is obviously delicious, as is cumin (and MSG powder), as is a little lime juice just at the end. To be honest, though, straight up salty and fried kale is a sensation as it is. Added to any sandwich, you have a salty and crunchy element that will elevate your already wonderful creation. This stuff is absolutely banging on top of a portion of chips from the chippie too.

PEA & LABNEH CROQUETTES

IT IS WORTH GIVING THIS CROQUETTE A SPECIAL MENTION. WE SERVED THESE IN THE SANDWICH SHOP AND THEY BLEW PEOPLE'S MINDS. THEY ARE SO SIMPLE TO MAKE. WE'VE GOT A LABNEH RECIPE ON PAGE 138 AND YOU'LL NEED TO MAKE SURE YOU'VE GOT SOME LABNEH IN THE HOUSE. BUT APART FROM THAT, THE LAST OF YOUR BAG OF FROZEN PEAS AND THE REMNANTS OF A JAR OF MINT SAUCE ARE ALL THAT YOU NEED TO PULL OFF THIS WIZARD.

100g labneh (see p.138)

2 tbsps mint sauce

100g frozen peas,
half blitzed to a mush,
half left whole

2 tbsps plain flour

2 medium eggs, beaten

150g dried white breadcrumbs (you want really dry bread blitzed up. See Ned Halley's Breadcrumbs p.218; alternatively use bought panko breadcrumbs, or ask the baker if they have some spare for you)

2 litres rapeseed oil

Find a mixing bowl and add the labneh, mint sauce and all the peas. Mix well and taste the mixture. It should be salty enough but adjust as you like. Put it in the fridge to get really cold.

Lay out your flour, beaten egg and breadcrumbs in three separate bowls.

Take a tablespoon of the mixture and drop first into the plain flour, then into the beaten egg and finally into the breadcrumbs. You should now have perfectly breaded little croquettes. Put them all back in the fridge to get nice and cold.

Heat the rapeseed oil in a high-sided pan, to 180°C. If you have a thermometer, use it and monitor the oil; alternatively, place a cube of stale bread in the pan and when it is fizzing and brown you are probably at peak oil temperature for frying.

Fry until golden and beautiful 3–4 at a time, as usual. These won't take long and nothing inside needs cooking so as soon as they're golden, whip 'em out and get them on kitchen roll! Enjoy with gay abandon, as usual. Preferably with white wine.

FRITTERS & BHAJIS

WHERE DOES A FRITTER END AND A BHAJI BEGIN? IN THE MIND OF THE BEHOLDER MY FRIEND, ONLY IN THEIR MIND.

FIND SOME NICE ROOT VEG, SOME ONIONS, SOME FLOUR, SOME WATER AND SOME SALT/PEPPER/SPICES/ETC. MIX THEM ABOUT AND FRY THE RESULTING MESS IN OIL – FRITTER/BHAJI/PAKORA/VADI/YOU NAME IT, YOU'VE JUST MADE IT. PLAIN FLOUR, SALT AND PEPPER MEANS THAT YOU'RE AT THE FRITTER END OF THE SPECTRUM; GRAM (CHICKPEA) FLOUR AND SOME CHILLI POWDER, YOU ARE AT THE BHAJI END. ADD SOME LENTILS AND SOME CORIANDER AND YOU'VE MADE A VADI. YOU'RE A GODDAMN GENIUS.

200g plain or gram (chickpea) flour

1 tbsp mixed spices (can be a combination of pepper, chilli powder, ground turmeric, fennel seeds, coriander seeds, ginger, caraway etc.) or leave this out altogether

1 tsp salt

1 red onion, sliced

3 carrots/beetroot/parsnips/turnips, etc., or a combination, about 200g in total

150ml sparkling water, cold

2 litres rapeseed oil

Start with the batter. Add the flour to a bowl and add any spices you intend on using. Experiment here and add whatever spices you fancy so that in total you have a tablespoon going in. Add the salt and mix together. Start slowly adding the sparkling water, whisking as you add it; once you have added half of it, there should be very few lumps in your batter. Keep adding the water until you have a single cream consistency. You might not need it all or you might need extra – just feel it out, be confident. If the batter seems too thin, add some more flour, if it seems too thick, add more water.

Next, slice the onion and grate your choice of root vegetables. Add these to the batter. Mix it with your hand and leave to sit for a minute.

Heat the rapeseed oil in a high-sided pan over a medium flame to 180°C. If you have a thermometer, use it and monitor the oil; alternatively, place a cube of stale bread in the pan and when it is fizzing and brown you are probably at peak oil temperature for frying.

When the oil reaches180°C carefully transfer tight handfuls of the mix to the hot oil. Do not overcrowd the pan. Fry for 2–3 minutes until golden brown and then drain on paper towel.

These can be any sandwich's nice crunchy element. The more spices you add, the more you should pair them with yogurt or labneh; the fewer you add, the more you should be thinking mayonnaise, piccalilli and lettuce. You get the gist. Have a look at The Bhaji Smuggler and The BJ Benton on p.34 and p.42 to see how we use bhaji/fritter type things at The Sandwich Shop.

FRIED ONIONS

Here is some good old-fashioned honesty for you. You can buy the most wonderful fried onions from food shops, supermarkets and Ikea. No one can be bothered to heat up oil, weep their way through a pile of onions, etc. Just go out and buy some crispy onions and add them to your sandwich.

DEEP FRIED SWEET POTATO STARCH NOODLES

I mean, what more could you want? These are worth making just for the sheer fun of it. You can see me discover these by accident (live on camera) in Episode 1 (Max's Korean Sarnie) of my *Vice* Munchies show, *The Sandwich Show*.

We're not going to give you a recipe. Heat some oil, to 180°C. Throw a clump of sweet potato starch noodles straight from the packet in their clear, vermicelli like form. Count to 10 and watch them expand, freak out and turn into thick, white, crispy, noodle-worms. Drain them on paper towel and hit them with salt, some chilli, some chaat masala, some lime zest, whatever you damn well fancy. Eat them as a snack, eat them in your sandwich, eat them for breakfast, do what you want. But make them, they are fun.

They are the mad looking white things in the picture of The Korean Gangster on p.37.

DEEP FRIED RAMEN NOODLES

We deep fry whole noodle cakes, from packets of instant ramen noodles from the supermarket, until they're golden brown. We leave them to cool and crush them on to the beef in the Korean Gangster sandwich (p. 37). These are a brilliant way of adding a lovely, toasty crunch to many sandwiches and they'll keep in an airtight container for as long as breadcrumbs.

BOMBAY MIX

Bombay Mix is one of the greatest things to ever go inside a sandwich. The crunch, the heat, the ethereal spicing, the crunch, did we mention the crunch.

If you want to make your own, perhaps Google it and watch a video, or buy the best Indian cookbook ever written, which is Pushpesh Pant's *India Cookbook*. For us, it isn't worth the drama; just go down the shops and buy a bag for a pound.

We use Bombay Mix in sandwiches at The Sandwich Shop (p.34) and as a crunchy topping for our potato dishes sometimes.

GARLIC CROUTONS

Take some old bread, with crusts or without, doesn't matter. Cut it up into small cubes, sugar lump size. Deep fry them. Or fry them in an inch of veg oil in a saucepan. Once golden and delicious like Greasy Spoon fried bread, take them out with a slotted spoon straight on to a plate covered with a paper towel and sprinkle liberally with garlic granules and toss them about. We use these in the "Et Tu Brute? Murdering The Caesar" (p.32) sandwich but they'd be good in tonnes of sarnies requiring some crunch. Feel free to experiment with other things from the spice rack sprinkled on them.

CASSAVA CHIPS

1 Cassava

2 litres rapeseed oil

Only buy firm, hard cassava. They should never be soft.

Peel the root and cut the top off and throw it away.

Slice into rounds as thin as you can. Ideally you'd use a mandolin, otherwise, you could use your veg peeler or your sharpest knife?

Heat the rapeseed oil in a high-sided pan over a medium flame to 190°C (375°F). If you have a thermometer, use it and monitor the oil; alternatively, place a cube of stale bread in the pan and when it is fizzing and brown you are probably at peak oil temperature for frying.

Deep fry the slices until golden brown and beautiful (oddly, they won't look dissimilar to slices of banana).

Take them out with a slotted spoon and put them onto a paper towel to cool and dry. At The Sandwich Shop we don't even put salt on them, but if you want them as a beer snack, salt while they are still hot.

These go SO well with beef in sandwiches (we use them in The Original Gangster p. 31). They are super crispy and sweet and the definition of earthy. When someone asks me what cassava tastes of, I normally say "it's like a super potato".

PANELLE

PANELLE (FROM SICILY), FARINATA (FROM LIGURIA) AND CECINA (FROM TUSCANY) ARE ALL THE SAME BLOODY THING AND ALL RIDICULOUSLY SIMPLE.

THEY ARE EASY TO MAKE AND DELICIOUS TO EAT. IT IS A NICHE PRODUCT, SO THIS MIGHT BE THE FIRST YOU ARE HEARING OF IT, AND IF SO, PLEASE TRY MAKING IT, AND PLEASE TRY PUTTING IT IN A SANDWICH. THE ITALIANS DO IT. NUFF SAID.

100g gram (chickpea) flour

350ml water

¼ tsp salt

75ml extra virgin olive oil

1 rosemary sprig (optional)

Preheat the oven to 200°C. Mix together the gram (chickpea) flour, water and salt to form a nice, smooth batter.

Heat the olive oil and the rosemary (if using) in a heavy-bottomed, ovenproof frying pan. Once the oil is proper hot and the rosemary is sizzling and beginning to brown, whip it out and add the batter. It will seem that there is a lot of oil in the pan – this is no bad thing and exactly what is supposed to happen. Allow the batter to sizzle and spit in the oil on the top of the stove for a minute before placing into the middle of the hot oven and cooking for a further 20 minutes until crispy and golden brown.

Remove from the oven and allow to cool slightly. Cut the panelle/farinata/cecina into pieces and eat or use as a filling in an Italian-inspired sandwich. It is entirely your call.

PICKLES
& THINGS

PICCALILLI

PICCALILLI IS ABSOLUTELY DELICIOUS, END OF, BUT IT DOES TAKE A LITTLE PREPARATION TO MAKE. IF YOU ARE STARING INTO A HAM AND CHEDDAR SANDWICH AS WE SPEAK AND YOU ARE THINKING HOW DELICIOUS THE ADDITION OF PICCALILLI WOULD BE, GO TO THE SUPERMARKET AND BUY SOME. BUT, WHILE YOU ARE THERE, WHY NOT PICK UP SOME VEGETABLES AND SPICES AS LISTED BELOW? BY THE TIME YOU HAVE FINISHED THAT JAR YOU ARE ABOUT TO PURCHASE, THE BATCH OF PICCALILLI THAT YOU ARE ABOUT TO MAKE WILL BE READY.

WE USE THIS VERY PICCALILLI RECIPE FOR THE STUFF WE MAKE TO GO IN THE HAM, EGG 'N' CHIPS (PAGE 26).

200g cauliflower or Romanesco cauliflower, leaves and all, cut into pea-sized chunks

200g broccoli, cut into pea-sized chunks

200g fine green beans, chopped into short lengths

200g carrots, peeled and grated

200g shallots, peeled and finely chopped

100g fennel, cut into pea-sized chunks

4 red chillies, halved, deseeded and finely chopped

50g salt

1 tsp cumin seeds

1 tsp coriander seeds

15g yellow mustard seeds

10g ground turmeric

10g English mustard powder

20g cornflour

600ml white wine vinegar

2 apples, grated

2 mangoes, peeled, stoned and roughly chopped

150g caster sugar

3 garlic cloves, crushed

2 tbsps dried oregano

4 bay leaves

3 x 750ml sterilised Kilner jars

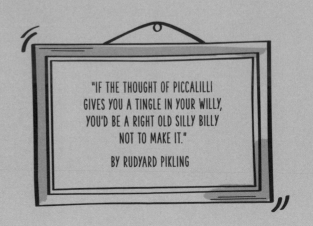

"IF THE THOUGHT OF PICCALILLI GIVES YOU A TINGLE IN YOUR WILLY, YOU'D BE A RIGHT OLD SILLY BILLY NOT TO MAKE IT."

BY RUDYARD PIKLING

As mentioned already, this recipe needs a little planning. You could cut up all the veg and whack it in a bowl in the fridge the day before because it is a mammoth task. Whether you chopped it yesterday or not, sprinkle the cut veg with the salt and use your hands to combine well. Cover with a tea towel or clingfilm and leave for 6–8 hours or overnight. When you are ready to make the piccalilli, drain the resulting liquid from the bowl, wash the veg well under cold running water and then sit in a sieve or colander to drip dry.

Meanwhile, in a spice grinder or using a pestle and mortar, add the cumin seeds, coriander seeds and mustard seeds and crush to a powder. Next add the turmeric, mustard powder and cornflour and grind together. Finally, add two tablespoons of the vinegar and mix into a loose paste.

Place a saucepan large enough to hold all your vegetables over a high heat and add the apple, mango, sugar, garlic, oregano, bay and remaining vinegar to the pan. Bring to the boil, stirring the mix occasionally to ensure that the fruit and sugar breaks down and dissolves. Once boiling, add the spice paste to the liquid and stir until it has completely combined. Simmer for 5 minutes and then remove from the heat.

Add all your vegetables to the hot spice goo and mix well. Cook for 15 minutes on a low heat, stirring gently but regularly, until the vegetables have just softened and started to release some juice. Spoon into sterilised jars and leave to cool. Once cool, make mini cartouches (p. 158) to press onto the top of the veg and store in the fridge for 3 weeks to a month before using. The wait will be worth it, trust us.

Sterilising Jars:

If you have a dishwasher, place your jar(s) and lid(s) in the machine (not attached to one another) and run on the hottest cycle you have. You can also bring a large pan of water to the boil and submerge the jars and their lids for a full minute in the boiling water. Do not try and dry the jars, simply place on a wire rack upside down to cool on their own.

LIME-PICKLED ONIONS

THESE ARE A PIECE OF PISS TO MAKE.

1 red onion, finely sliced

Juice of 1 lime

½ tsp Salt

Put the sliced onion in a bowl, squeeze over the lime, add the salt and cover with clingfilm. If the lime is hard, roll it firmly on a board with the flat of your palm to break down the internal structure of the lime and give you more juice when squeezing.

Mix well, cover with clingfilm and allow to sit for at least 3 hours, or up to a week. If you're playing the short game, shake the bowl every half an hour or so. Long game? Shake the bowl once a day for a week. The longer they're in there the more neon pink and lip-puckering they will become. Just look at the ones in The Spaniard on p.28. You can now use them in any sandwich requiring a sour kick.

Sometimes they start to ferment and fizz a little, which is nothing bad, in fact it's rather fun and they're still delicious.

You could perhaps add a sliced chilli (jalapeño?) in there too for a kick of heat.

VERY LIGHTLY PICKLED ONIONS

These take about half an hour and are a wonderful addition to salads and many sandwiches that want the freshness of onion but not the astringency. We use them in The Original Gangster (see p.31) combined with loads of parsley.

Top and tail an onion and slice it as thin as you can the "wrong way" from tip to base, not across its body as usual. Onions cut like this give in more readily and cook down much quicker if you're making onion soup or something. Put your onion slices in a plastic container like an old yoghurt pot or a little Tupperware box. Sprinkle them with salt and squeeze half a lemon on them, shake them about with a lid on and leave for half an hour. Done.

SAUERKRAUT

THERE ARE DECENT BRANDS OF SAUERKRAUT IN THE SHOPS, BUT IT'S SUCH FUN TO DO A BIT OF FERMENTING YOURSELF.

1 white cabbage,
very finely sliced

1 tbsp salt

100ml water (if you need it)

1 x 750ml sterilised Kilner jar

This takes 10 days. If you have a dishwasher, place your Kilner jar and lid in the machine and run on the hottest cycle. You can also boil a large pan of water and submerge the jar and the lid for a full minute. Do not dry them, place them on a wire rack upside down to cool on their own.

Add half the cabbage and half the salt to a mixing bowl. Get your hands in and massage and scrunch the cabbage. It will begin to break down and release some liquid. Perfect. Add the rest of the cabbage and salt to the bowl and get in there again. Once the cabbage has wilted , and there's plenty of liquid sloshing about, start to fill your kilner jar. Fist the cabbage down so that it releases more moisture and is well compressed in the jar. You will get it all in there.

Add any remaining water from the bowl. If you need a little extra to completely cover it add some tap water. If your cabbage was nice and juicy you shouldn't need it, but you want the cabbage completely submerged.

Leave the lid of the kilner jar ajar, and cover with a tea towel. Leave in a cool dark place for 10 days. Check on it intermittently, making sure it is still submerged and adding a little water if not. Do not be alarmed at a little white froth or if the cabbage changes colour – this is normal. Taste your kraut with a fork throughout to get a sense of how it changes and where in the process you like it best.

Always get the cabbage out with a fork, fingers bring unwanted guests to the pickle party!

After 10 days, close the lid and store it in the fridge. Enjoy as and when you have a sandwich that might benefit from its inclusion. This will keep for an eternity.

If you are a tinkerer, feel free to add spices (caraway is a classic), slices of red chilli or grated carrot etc. to your kraut. Follow the process above and experiment your way to heaven.

KIMCHI

HERE IS THE PROBLEM WITH KIMCHI: IT IS A SERIOUS BUSINESS, AND MANY PEOPLE WOULD SAY DON'T MESS WITH IT. IT'S FUN TO MAKE SOMETHING LIKE THIS AT HOME THOUGH ISN'T IT?! IT'S A WONDERFUL LITTLE PROJECT. SO, IF YOU WOULD LIKE TO TRY AND MAKE KIMCHI, HERE IS A MONSTER RECIPE. REMEMBER, IN KOREA IT IS SEEN ALMOST AS A CONDIMENT. EATEN ALONGSIDE MANY, IF NOT MOST, THINGS TO ADD A BIT OF OOMPH.

2 Chinese cabbages

120g salt

4 garlic cloves

A lump of ginger the size of a Mars Bar

2 pears, grated

1 bunch of spring onions, roughly chopped

1 bunch of radishes, sliced

2 tbsps dried chilli flakes , gochugaru are the Korean ones if you can find them, or use normal chilli flakes

2 tbsps fish sauce

1 tbsp doenjang paste

1 tbsp dried shrimps

1 pinch cayenne pepper

1 tsp shrimp paste

100g caster sugar

100ml white wine vinegar

First, you must salt the cabbage. Stand each cabbage on its base and cut down 90 per cent of the way down through the cabbage, turn it 90 degrees and cut again. You should have almost quartered it. Open up the cuts and liberally salt. Next, submerge these salted cabbages in water and leave in the fridge overnight. The next morning, rinse under fresh running water and put aside.

Find your food processor, and add every other ingredient on the list. Blitz to a smooth-ish paste.

Take the recently rinsed cabbages and stuff the mixture evenly between the leaves of the cabbage. You literally want to peel each leaf apart and with your fingers smear a bit of spicy mixture in there. Once you have used all your mix and have well-stuffed cabbages, place them in an airtight, non-metallic container and put the lid on – well and liberally applied clingfilm will work perfectly, round and round the container.

Store for 5 days in a cool, dark place, turning the kimchi over every day. After 5 days you will have a tasty, slightly funky kimchi. If you want more funk, then go longer. If you are happy, then store it in the fridge until you have a sandwich underway that wants some sour, spicy, cabbagey funk in it.

We often use Kimchi, sometimes mixed with sauerkraut, in our beef sandwiches, like the Korean Gangster on (p.37).

Chop some of this up and slap it in anywhere you want.

DILL PICKLES

YOU'VE STOPPED PICKING THE GHERKINS OUT OF YOUR CHEESEBURGER HAVEN'T YOU?! THEY'RE THE BEST BLOODY BIT!! WELL GUESS WHAT, THEY ARE SO EASY TO MAKE YOU'LL BE CRYING TEARS OF JOY THE NEXT TIME YOU'RE MAKING A SARNIE FOR YOUR TEA WITH RICH MEATY LEFTOVERS AND YOU'RE DESPERATE FOR SOMETHING SHARP AND CRUNCHY TO COMPLIMENT IT ALL.

1kg small cucumbers (about the length of a Mars Bar, you'll likely need to visit a proper greengrocer for these)

6 garlic cloves

1 tbsp fennel seeds

½ bunch of dill

300ml white wine vinegar

300ml water

3 tbsps caster sugar

1 x 750ml sterilised Kilner jar or 5–6 smaller jars

This recipe makes a pretty decent batch of pickles, which is handy as they are insanely good to eat, and, if you properly sanitise your jars prior to making, they will last until the second coming.

If you have a dishwasher, place your jar(s) and lid(s) in the machine (not attached to one another) and run on the hottest cycle you have. You can also bring a large pan of water to the boil and submerge the jar(s) and their lids for a full minute in the boiling water. Do not try and dry the jars, simply place on a wire rack upside down to cool on their own.

Next, the pickles. You can leave your little cucumbers whole (do trim off any little tails they may have though) or quarter them, sliced lengthways, or chop them into little rounds. Either way, pack them into your jar/jars once sterilised. My favourite is slices so they're straight up ready for sandwiching.

Divide the garlic, fennel seeds, and dill between the jars and leave to one side while you make your pickling liquor.

Take a saucepan and place over a medium heat. Add the vinegar, water, and sugar and bring to the boil. Allow to simmer for 1 minute or until the sugar and salt has dissolved. Take off the heat and leave until warm, not hot. Pour the warm liquor over the cucumbers in their jars. Knock and bang your jars about a bit to make sure the brine has settled all the way down and that there are no air bubbles and nothing poking out the liquid. Top up with any excess brine if needs be.

Leave on the side to cool, and once at room temperature, seal with the lid and place in the fridge. If you want these to last for a millennia, you can pasteurise the sealed pickle jars by running them (with their lids on and everything) through a dishwasher cycle again or dropping them back into a pan of boiling water for another 5 minutes. Personally, we eat these so quickly there is no need for any pasteurisation, but if you're a slow coach, pasteurise and be content with your pickle situation for decades to come.

And remember to NEVER put your fingers in the pickle jar! Always use a fork or something to get them out. Fingers means gatecrashers will very likely take over the pickle party.

PICKLED EGGS

EVER SINCE WE WERE INTRODUCED, AS CHILDREN, TO THE JOYS OF A PICKLED EGG IN A BAG OF CRISPS (AND LATTERLY A PINT OF CIDER) AT THE SEYMOUR ARMS WE'VE BEEN HOOKED!

6 medium eggs (slightly older eggs are better here as fresh eggs are a devil to peel)

200ml malt vinegar

100ml water

1 tbsp Salt

1 shallot, sliced

4 whole black peppercorns

1 x 750ml sterilised Kilner jar

If you have a dishwasher, place your jar(s) and lid(s) in the machine (not attached to one another) and run on the hottest cycle you have. You can also bring a large pan of water to the boil and submerge the jars and their lids for a full minute in the boiling water. Do not try and dry the jars, simply place on a wire rack upside down to cool on their own.

Cover the eggs with cold water in a saucepan and bring to the boil over a high heat. As soon as the water is boiling, remove from the heat and allow to cool in the water. When the eggs are at room temperature, peel them and place in a large jar to be well and truly pickled.

Next, combine the vinegar, water, salt, shallot and peppercorns in a pan and bring to a rolling boil. Pour this immediately over the eggs, ensuring that all the eggs are properly submerged. Allow to cool before refrigerating for 2-3 days before serving.

If you want spicy pickled eggs, add some whole chillies (those red ones from the shop) to your pickling liquor when you bring it to the boil. Similarly exciting is the addition of a few slices of pickled beetroot (or some of the liquid from a jar of supermarket pickled beetroot) to the eggs. This will give you bright pink pickled eggs!!!

PICKLED CHILLIES

SOMETIMES YOU JUST WANT A SPICY, VINEGARY, SWEET-AND-SOUR KICK IN YOUR SANDWICH. WELL, IF YOU HAVE THESE LITTLE FIRECRACKERS AT THE BACK OF YOUR FRIDGE NEXT TO A PARTIALLY-SQUEEZED TUBE OF TOMATO PURÉE, YOU WILL BE THE HAPPIEST SANDWICH MAKER IN THE WORLD.

150g long, green chillies
(Turkish style is best)

200ml white wine vinegar

1 tbsp salt

50g caster sugar

1 x 750ml sterilised Kilner jar

If you have a dishwasher, place your jar(s) and lid(s) in the machine (not attached to one another) and run on the hottest cycle you have. You can also bring a large pan of water to the boil and submerge the jars and their lids for a full minute in the boiling water. Do not try and dry the jars, simply place on a wire rack upside down to cool on their own.

Prick your chillies with a toothpick or the tip of a sharp knife a few times. You want these wicked vinegary, and you want the vinegar to seep inside the chilli, giving you a mouthful of spicy vinegar when you bite into it.

Pack the whole chillies into the jar and leave to one side.

Heat the vinegar, salt and sugar over a medium heat and, when boiling, pour immediately over the chillies. Allow to cool to room temp, cover with a lid, place in the fridge and use one day in a sandwich.

SUMAC-PICKLED PEPPERS

Sumac is a boss. A little berry that is picked, dried and ground and then packs a smoky, citrus punch that lemons can only dream of.

You want to follow the recipe above, but add two tablespoons of sumac powder to the pickling liquor once it has cooled. And rather than chillies, you need those nice long paler green Turkish peppers (sometimes called finger peppers). The ones that aren't spicy. Otherwise, proceed as the recipe suggests. The only difference is that when you come to serve them, or use them, you want to toss them through with a little finely sliced onion, some coriander, and a liberal pinch or two of sumac. Find your level, it is underwhelming if you don't use enough, and overpowering if you use too much.

NO CREDIT

MAX'S SANDW

SUPER AMAZING
DUCK PL
£20

For Duck

MAX'S SA

LET'S
HAVE
A

PICKLED GRAPES

THESE ARE FROM THE "ET TU BRUTE? MURDERING THE CAESAR SANDWICH" (PAGE 32). AND THEY ARE TOTALLY AND UTTERLY DELICIOUS. TRY THESE IN NEARLY EVERY SANDWICH YOU MAKE JUST TO SEE IF IT WORKS.

200ml white wine vinegar

100ml water

100ml caster sugar

1 big bunch of seedless grapes, white or red, washed, picked and halved

1 x 750ml sterilised Kilner jar

If you have a dishwasher, place your jar(s) and lid(s) in the machine (not attached to one another) and run on the hottest cycle you have. You can also bring a large pan of water to the boil and submerge the jars and their lids for a full minute in the boiling water. Do not try and dry the jars, simply place on a wire rack upside down to cool on their own.

Bring all the ingredients (apart from the grapes) up to the boil and allow to go cold.

Put the grapes in the kilner jar and cover with the cooled liquid. These will be ready in only a few hours.

PICKLED APRICOTS

200ml white wine vinegar

100ml water

100g caster sugar

250g dried apricots

As above sunshine, as above, but leave the apricots whole. These are from Tom Oldroyd's Curried Lamb Sandwich (p.40) and they need at least a day in the liquid before you have a try.

SIDES

& OTHER TINGS

MAC & CHEESE BALLS

This will make about 12 balls:

150g 'elbow' macaroni (we use de cecco chifferi rigati)

40g butter

40g plain flour, sieved

300ml full fat milk

100g mature cheddar, grated

25g pickled jalapeño slices, incredibly finely chopped

1 level tsp Salt

For the crumb:

4 medium eggs whisked up, in a large bowl

4 heaped tbsps flour, on a nice big plate

A plate covered in breadcrumbs (p.218)

2 litres rapeseed oil

This seems like a tiny amount of jalapeño, but it's one of those "when it's not there you miss it" things.

Cook the pasta to very nearly cooked but not quite (al dente), in plenty of well-salted, boiling water. Drain it and put it in a container that is big enough to hold lashings of sauce too.

Now, get your whisk out, you're going to make béchamel. Melt the butter in a pan on a medium heat. Add the flour, stirring all the time and cook until it smells biscuity and no longer of raw flour (this will take 2–5 minutes and don't let it burn). It might go a bit brown, don't be worried. Biscuits are brown.

Slowly begin to add the milk, about 50ml at a time, whisking vigorously all the time. The vigour of your whisking will help to ensure an even dispersal of the flour throughout the liquid, keeping it lump free. This is also why a whisk is better than a wooden spoon. Once it's all in there, you should have a nice smooth, creamy looking sauce.

Add the cheese, jalapeño and salt. Stir stir stir. Once the cheese has completely melted, pour the sauce on the pasta and mix it all thoroughly. Allow the whole lot to cool and set (this will take at least 2 hours, maybe more).

Using your hands, grab a lump of the cold mixture and roll it about in your hands into a ball(ish). Rough balls are fine. Don't worry about making it too smooth. We make them about 40g – roughly the size of a ping pong ball.

Once they're all rolled they need to be panéd, which means floured, egged and breadcrumbed.

Put a ball in the flour on the plate and roll it about until it's coated. Now put it in the egg and do the same. Now into the breadcrumbs and roll it about the same. Repeat. You can do more than one at a time, but probably not more than 4. You might need to top up the flour, egg and breadcrumbs.

Heat the rapeseed oil in a high-sided pan over a medium flame to 190°C. If you have a thermometer, use it and monitor the oil; alternatively, place a cube of stale bread in the pan and when it is fizzing and brown you are probably at peak oil temperature for frying.

Fry the balls about 5 at a time until golden and beautiful, about 3 minutes is probably perfect and will make sure the inside is all gooey and sexy.

ARANCINI

GO READ MARCELLA HAZAN, GIORGIO LOCATELLI, RACHEL RODDY, THE RIVER CAFÉ, OR EVEN SIGNOR JAMIE OLIVER, AND TEACH YOURSELF HOW TO MAKE RISOTTO, THAT IS NOT OUR BATTLE.

ARANCINI ARE AN ABSOLUTE DELIGHT WHEN MADE AND EATEN FRESH. THEY CAN BE A NIGHTMARE WHEN LIBERATED FROM A 4-HOUR SENTENCE UNDER A HEAT LAMP IN A QUESTIONABLE ITALIAN CAFÉ. SO MAKE THEM FRESH.

4 tbsps plain flour

100g breadcrumbs
(like Ned Halley's on p.218)

2 medium eggs, beaten

400g cooked and cooled risotto, preferably leftover – what sort of savage would make risotto just to make arancini?

1 ball of buffalo mozzarella,

4 tsps leftover tomato sauce, or a good passata

2 litres rapeseed oil

Lay out your flour, breadcrumbs and beaten egg in three separate bowls. You are going to *pane*, so be prepared.

Take a palmful of the risotto and flatten out into 5mm thickness in said palm – a rough circle will do. Place a teaspoon of tomato sauce and a 10-pence-sized piece of mozzarella in the middle. Gently close your palm around the fillings, using your free hand to bring the sticky risotto up around the filling. You can use a little extra risotto if needed to get a good seal at the top.

Do this for all of your risotto until you have 6–8 nice neat balls, all filled, all ready.

Roll each ball first in the flour, then in the egg and then in the breadcrumbs so that the arancini is completely coated. Once you are happy, if you can wait, refrigerate the balls for 30 minutes or more.

Place the oil in a high-sided pan and warm it over a medium flame. If you have a thermometer, use it and monitor the oil until it reaches 180°C or until a piece of bread dropped inside browns within 20 seconds.

Finally, drop the arancini 2–3 at a time into the hot oil and fry until perfectly pecan brown. Drain on paper towels with a light sprinkling of salt. Wait at least 5 minutes until you eat them. That mozzarella and tomato sauce is a burnt lip waiting to happen.

LASAGNE BALLS

LIKE THE ARANCINI, THERE IS NO CHANCE WE'RE BOTHERING WITH A RECIPE FOR LASAGNE. YOU ALREADY HAVE A RECIPE FOR LASAGNE, YOU MAKE IT ALL THE TIME, YOU KNOW WHAT YOU'RE DOING. NEXT TIME YOU'RE MAKING IT, MAKE EXTRA. COZ YOU ARE GOING TO WANT TO MAKE SOME OF THESE.

4 tbsps plain flour

100g breadcrumbs
(like Ned Halley's on p.218)

2 medium eggs, beaten

400g cold, cooked lasagne, cut into small cubes and put back in the fridge to go really cold

2 litres rapeseed oil

Salt

Lay out your flour, breadcrumbs and beaten egg in three separate bowls.

Take a square of lasagne and drop it in the flour. Try your best to keep it together and roll it around (the colder they are the less likely they are to fall apart). Next, pop the floured lasagne square into the egg and roll it about. You can use a fork if you like. Finally, drop it into the breadcrumbs and completely cover it in the offending crumbs. Repeat for all the lasagne you have.

Now you're ready to fry. Place the oil in a high-sided pan and warm it over a medium flame. If you have a thermometer, use it and monitor the oil until it reaches 180°C or until a piece of bread dropped inside browns within 20 seconds. Or heat 1cm of veg oil in a decent frying pan and fry them in there.

Drop the crumbed lasagne into the hot oil and fry until golden brown. You want to do this 3–4 at a time. Once golden, drain on paper towels and sprinkle with salt.

Go to heaven.

CAULIFLOWER CHEESE BALLS

ARE YOU GOING TO WANT A RECIPE FOR CAULIFLOWER CHEESE? YOU ARE, AREN'T YOU.
OK, BUT IT'S GOING TO BE ROUGH AND READY, AND QUICK, SO PAY ATTENTION.

1 head of cauliflower. All the cauliflower's arms are delicious too. So sweet and so crunchy. Cut them up and whack 'em in a salad or something

50g butter

50g plain flour

500ml milk

Grated cheese of your choice

For the balls

4 tbsps plain flour

100g breadcrumbs (like Ned Halley's on p.218)

2 medium eggs, beaten

400g (ish) leftover cauliflower cheese, from the fridge, as cold as possible (from the outstanding recipe above)

2 litres rapeseed oil

Maldon sea salt

Preheat the oven to 200°C. Take the cauliflower, dig out the stalk with a knife and break the head into nice small florets. Use as much force as necessary to break the bastard up. Melt the butter in a pan on a low-ish heat. Add the flour and stir it all about until it mixes and makes a paste, watch the heat, keep it low, cook for about 3 minutes until it has a faint, biscuity aroma. A whisk is preferable to a wooden spoon here if you've got one. Add a splash of the milk and stir into the flour and butter mix; add a splash more, stir again, add a larger splash, stir well and you should have a nice saucy sauce, so add the rest of the milk and stir or whisk to a smooth sauce. Add the cauliflower florets into the sauce and cook for 4 minutes on a low simmer before transferring to a baking tray and covering LIBERALLY in some grated cheese (Cheddar, Comte, Beaufort, Parmesan, etc., all work well, but use whatever cheese you have, experiment). Place in the hot oven and cook for 35–40 minutes until the top is browned and the cauliflower is soft. Eat whilst still hot, perhaps followed by a well dressed salad made from the arms? And make sure you save some leftovers for your cauliflower cheese balls.

For the balls: Lay out your flour, breadcrumbs and beaten egg in three separate bowls.

Take a tbsp of the leftover cauliflower cheese and drop it in the flour. Try your best to keep it cohesive and roll it in flour. As with the lasagne balls, the colder the cauliflower cheese is the better. Next, pop it in the beaten egg and roll it about. Finally, drop it into the breadcrumbs and completely cover it in them. Repeat for all the leftover cauliflower you have and put it back in the fridge.

Now you're ready to fry, so heat your rapeseed oil to 180°C in a large, high-sided saucepan.

Drop the crumbed balls into the hot oil and fry until golden brown. You want to do this 3–4 at a time. Once golden, drain on paper towels and sprinkle with salt.

DEEP FRIED CAULIFLOWER

SHOULD THIS HAVE BEEN IN THE VEG SECTION? PROBABLY, BUT IT WAS TOO LATE, WE COULDN'T CHANGE IT HAHAHAHHA.

THE IDEA FOR THESE CAME FROM A SANDWICH DESIGNED FOR US BY TOM OLDROYD (PAGE 40) AND HE IS A FLAVOUR NINJA. THESE LIGHTLY SPICED, FRIED CAULIFLOWER PIECES ARE THE WORK OF A TWISTED MIND, AND THAT SHOULD BE ALL THE ENCOURAGEMENT YOU NEED TO MAKE THESE AND SANDWICH WITH THEM. ESPECIALLY WHEN YOU'VE LEFTOVER CURRY.

½ head cauliflower, broken into small 1cm florets

1 litre rapeseed oil

1 tsp salt, plus extra to serve

2 tsps ground turmeric

1 tsp chilli powder

2 tsps cornflour

Start by mixing your cauliflower florets, 1 tbsp of the rapeseed oil, salt, turmeric, chilli powder and cornflour in a bowl so that each floret is completely covered in clumps of tasty spicing.

Heat the rest of the rapeseed oil in a high-sided pan until it reaches 180°C. Carefully drop the coated florets one handful at a time into the hot oil. Fry until golden and crispy (roughly 1–2 minutes) and then remove to drain on some paper towels with a good pinch of salt.

CHICKEN WINGS

Who doesn't love chicken wings? That's what Tom Mcsweeney said and they've been on the menu ever since.

We cut ours into their individual parts, the little drumsticks and the bits with two bones in, and marinate them in a 50/50 mix of light soy sauce and white wine vinegar. You could do it in a tub or a Tupperware box with a nice tight lid giving it a shake every now and again.

We leave them in the liquid for 2 days in the fridge so they pickle and brine.

When they are ordered, we roll them in a 50/50 mix of flour (the one we use to make the bread, p.114) and Smash (yup, that's right, the instant mash potato powder) and deep fry them at 180°C for 6 minutes. At home you can by all means deep fry them, or just shallow fry them (in a centimetre of oil), turning occasionally until all sides are a deep, golden brown.

We then slather them in Guindilla Yoghurt (see p.152), and put Lime-Pickled Onions (see p.232) on top, along with their best mate, the thinly sliced green bits of spring onions.

CRUSHED FRIED POTATOES

Cut unpeeled potatoes into large pieces of similar sizes and boil them until really soft and nearly falling apart. Drain in a colander and leave to steam until cold. When you want to deep fry them, crush them with your hands so you have pieces of all sizes, some big, some tiny, some just skins. When we fish them out the fryer, we season them immediately with salt and spices as it says below here. My favourite is tossing them in sumac and salt then dunking them in the Harissa Yoghurt on p.148.

FLAVOURED SALTS

Whatever powder you might be mixing the salt with, go 50/50. We've done sumac, curry powder and tonnes of other stuff! They're all great sprinkled on crunchy fried potatoes and tossed about in a bowl before being dunked into something sexy.

SALADS

THE ONLY SALAD YOU'LL EVER NEED

The best dressing for all and every salad is lemon juice and olive oil. No mustard, no garlic, no nothing. One-third lemon juice, two-thirds olive oil, salt and pepper, and whisk, whisk, whisk into an emulsion or shake it all up in a jar. You're done.

When Ben and I used to work at a restaurant called LeCoq people often asked "Oh my god, this salad, what IS the dressing?" It was lemon juice and olive oil.

Salad is an integral part of many of the sandwiches at The Sandwich Shop. Nothing adds crunchy freshness like crunchy fresh things.

I'm loathed to give you a salad recipe. Use whatever tickles your fancy. At The Sandwich Shop we mostly use either a mix of chopped baby gem lettuce and chicory, with other things added or we just use herbs. Parsley, mint and dill in equal quantities and dressed as usual is a firm favourite.

Having a Sunday roast? Make a salad by pickling the leaves from whole bunches of parsley and mint, and snipping a whole bunch of dill up with scissors. Dressed as usual, this is one of the most wonderful salads in the world.

Baby Gem (leaves left whole or perhaps torn in half) and rocket is also wonderful. Whatever you've got lying about: onions, spring onions, carrots, cucumbers, beetroots or tomatoes, random pickles, they're all delicious. Chop them up small, make them into strips with your vegetable peeler if they're hard, mix them together in a bowl and dress as above.

Sometimes we use things like capers, caper berries or chopped gherkins in our salads for extra zing and crunch. My favourite is sliced up guindillas (pickled Spanish chillies, like kebab shop chillies). Sometimes crispy bits of bacon have been known to make it into my salads, leftover lentils and grilled bread as in Ben's wonderful recipe just by this one. There are no rules; it's bloody salad, not tax law.

BREAD SALAD – THE ONLY OTHER SALAD YOU'LL EVER NEED

THIS IS A TWIST ON THE INFAMOUS PANZANELLA.

IF YOU ENJOY THE ONE BELOW, MAKE IT AGAIN, BUT SUBSTITUTE THE BITTER SALAD LEAVES WITH TOMATOES. DON'T GRILL THEM, JUST CUT 'EM UP AND LATHER WITH THE SALT AND THE VINEGAR AND OIL, ETC.

1 head bitter salad leaf, quartered (chicory, endive, radicchio, etc.)

150g leftover bread, cut into large cubes

2 tbsps extra virgin olive oil

2 tbsps red wine vinegar

Salt

1 tbsp pine nuts
(any roughly chopped nut would work equally well)

1 tbsp capers (optional)

Some sweet herbs, torn (tarragon, mint, parsley, oregano, etc. all work well – a comnbination of whatever you have is perfect)

Preheat the oven to 200°C.

Take your cubes of bread and toss them with 1 tablespoon of the olive oil and 1 teaspoon of the salt. Stick them in a tray in the hot oven and cook for 8–10 minutes until they are golden and crunchy.

Meanwhile, heat a dry frying pan over a high flame and when stinking hot, press the quarters of bitter salad into the pan. You want scorch and singe and sizzle. Turn and do the same to all sides. When limp and a little burnt, remove from the pan and lay on a plate. Dress with the remaining oil, vinegar, salt, pine nuts, capers and torn herbs. It can sit like this in a pile whilst you wait for the bread to finish crisping.

When ready to serve, place the bread in a bowl and pour in all the excess juice that has settled on the plate from the burnt salad and the oil, etc. Mix this into the bread and give a cheeky one-two-scrunch with your hands. Now add the salad, herbs, nuts, etc. and mix well. Taste it, you'll almost certainly want more vinegar, and perhaps a bit more salt, and definitely some more oil. Mix again, taste again, repeat until blissfully happy or the salad has all but disappeared. This works as an accompaniment or indeed as the filling to a left-field sandwich. Mmmmmmmm.

X'S 2014

M

ZONE
urant

@LUNCHEON

HOT
SANDWICHES
== & ==
BOOZE!

PUDDINGS

CHOUX BUNS (WHAT YOU FILL WITH CREAM AND CALL A PROFITEROLE)

CHOUX BETTER BELIEVE IT.

120ml water

100g butter, cubed

20g caster sugar

A tiny pinch of salt

120g plain flour, sieved

4 medium eggs

Combine the water, butter, sugar and salt in a heavy-bottomed saucepan and place over a medium heat. Melt the butter and bring the liquid to a near simmer, but do not allow the mixture to boil – that is imperative. Shoot in the flour as quickly as possible (by putting it all in a folded sheet of greaseproof paper and dumping it into the pan in one go) and beat well with a wooden spoon until you have a dough that is flinging its way about your pan. Lower the heat and cook this dough for 3–4 minutes to ensure that the raw taste of flour is cooked out.

Remove the pan from the heat and crack in the eggs one by one. This will mess with your hitherto perfect-looking dough, but don't be alarmed. Beat the egg in vigorously each time, until the dough comes back together. It will come back together, we promise you.

When all the eggs are in, allow the dough to continue cooling before storing in the fridge until you are ready to use it.

Preheat the oven to 200°C.

Fill a piping bag with the pastry mix and line a baking tray with greaseproof paper. The old trick of a bit oil underneath will make the paper stick down perfectly. The easiest way to pipe these is to pick a ball you like, say a golf ball. Use it as your reference. Put pressure on the piping bag so that the choux is coming out and pipe confidently on one spot until the choux is about the size you had envisaged. Stop putting pressure on the bag and whip it up and away, leaving you with a perfectly piped mound of choux. You can use a tablespoon dipped in cold water to portion the pastry (instead of the piping bag) but the end result will be more rustic, which might not be a bad thing.

Do this again and again until you have a tray of identical choux buns. Get a little water and, with a wet finger, round off any flicks or peaks of choux on the top of each bun. It should be round and smooth on top. The peaks or flicks will burn in the oven if you do not do this.

The cooking is perhaps the most technical bit, although it is actually very simple. Place the buns in the centre of the hot oven and close the door. Immediately turn the temperature down to 170°C and cook for 10 minutes. Turn the temperature down again to 120°C and cook for another 10 minutes. Now turn the oven off and leave for a further 10 minutes. Do not open the oven door in all this time. Once the cooking is finished, remove the choux buns from the oven and cool on a wire rack.

You could fill these with any number of different creams, custards, curds, god knows what. Once they've gone cold, we chop them in half and whack a ball of ice cream in there.

MACARONS

LORDY, DAWDY, SOMEONE LIKES TO PARTY. YOU THOUGHT YOU WERE BUYING A WHIMSICAL BOOK ABOUT SANDWICHES, AND HERE YOU ARE MAKING THE PASTRY CHEF'S NEMESIS LIKE THE BREEZE ON A SPRING MORNING. AND WHY THE FUCK NOT? THERE IS NO TWO WAYS ABOUT IT, MACARONS ARE HARD TO MAKE AND NEED PRECISION AND PATIENCE. IF YOU ARE UP FOR IT, THEN SO ARE WE. I MEAN, AN ICE CREAM SANDWICH MADE WITH MACARONS IS MIND-BLOWING – THE CLOSEST THING YOU WILL HAVE TO A SEXUAL EXPERIENCE IN THE KITCHEN WITHOUT SMEARING MAYONNAISE ALL OVER YOURSELF. BUT, AND IT IS A BIG BUT, YOU MAY WELL BE BETTER OFF JUST BUYING SOME IF YOU ARE AT ALL SHORT-TEMPERED, SENSITIVE, OR SIMPLY HAVE BETTER THINGS TO DO THAN SPENDING THE NEXT 24 HOURS IN A MACARON-INDUCED PANIC.

120g egg whites
(from old eggs at room
temperature)

¼ tsp salt

50g caster sugar

¼ tsp cream of tartar

Natural food colouring
of your choice

200g icing sugar

120g ground almonds

First, you want to use an electric whisk or KitchenAid type thing to whisk your eggs on a high-speed to a nice froth. After a minute or two, add the salt, whisk for a minute more and then slowly add the sugar and cream of tartar while you continue to whisk. After 5 or so minutes of whisking, you should have nice stiff peaks. At this point, add a food colouring of your choice to turn the eventual macaron from beigey-white to pink, green, red, etc. A few drops of a natural food colouring should do it, but if you want a nice, vivid colour, sneak in a few more drops.

Next you will need to very carefully fold in the icing sugar and ground almonds. This will take some time, and if not done properly, it can ruin your macarons. The key is to be careful and patient. Do not beat the mix in any way. Cut and fold your spoon though the mixture, turning the bowl by 90° each time. You want to maintain all the volume you have put into the mix with the whisking.

Preheat the oven to 180°C.

Once well folded, transfer the mixture to a piping bag. You need to cover a completely flat baking tray with greaseproof paper. Remember our old trick of a touch of oil underneath, which will stick it down perfectly. Next you'll need to pipe 4–5cm rounds of mixture onto your baking tray, leaving each macaron at least 2cm apart on the tray. Once you have done this, lift up the tray and drop it from about 15cm onto your kitchen surface. Do this about 3 or 4 times. This is a crucial step as it knocks out any air bubbles in the mix and means your macarons will cook perfectly. Finally, leave the tray of macarons uncovered on the side for 30 minutes. This allows a skin to form on the macarons and will again ensure a perfect cook.

Finally, place the tray in the oven and bake for 12 minutes. Open the door of your oven at two specific moments, and this is essential. Once at 8 minutes and again at 11 minutes. Open, breath, breathe again, and close the door. At 12 minutes, remove from the oven and slide the greaseproof paper with the macarons on it onto a cool surface. Leave them for 10 minutes before lifting them off the paper and cooling on a wire rack.

At this juncture, you are going to be smug and difficult to be around. So perhaps take some time alone with your macarons before you share your triumph with anyone else. Finally, fill your macarons with an ice cream of your choice and share them with the people you love the most.

COOKIES

IF YOU KNOW WHAT IS GOOD FOR YOU, YOU WILL HAVE A ROLL OF THIS COOKIE DOUGH IN YOUR FREEZER AT ALL TIMES. IT MEANS YOU ARE NEVER MORE THAN 20 MINUTES AWAY FROM FRESHLY BAKED COOKIES, AND THAT YOU CAN INDULGE YOURSELF WITH AN ICE CREAM SANDWICH ANY TIME OF DAY OR NIGHT.

150g salted butter,
at room temperature

100g light brown sugar

50g caster sugar

1 egg

240g plain flour

50g cocoa powder

½ tsp bicarbonate of soda

100g dark chocolate chips

1 tsp sea salt flakes,
the expensive stuff

Preheat your oven to 170°C and line a baking tray with greaseproof paper.

Start by creaming together the butter and sugars with a wooden spoon (or with an electric whisk) until light and fluffy. Add the egg and beat well before stirring in the flour, cocoa powder and bicarbonate of soda. Do not overwork the dough – as soon as it has come together, stop. Add the choc chips and mix a few more times to distribute. Turn out onto a sheet of greaseproof paper and use your hands to form the mix into a sausage about 7cm (in diameter). Roll this up in the greaseproof, twist the ends like an old-fashioned sweet, and place in the freezer for 30 minutes.

To cook the cookies, slice a few 1cm thick rounds from your sausage and place these a few centimetres apart on some more greaseproof paper, on your baking tray. Sprinkle each cookie with a few sea salt flakes as this will enhance the chocolatey taste. Place in the hot oven and cook for 13 minutes.

Remove from the oven and allow to cool on the tray. Do not be alarmed that they look soft – they will continue to cook while they cool and this is how we get that soft-centred-perfection that we are after.

Once you have your cookie, the world is your oyster. We recommend doubling them over a ball of ice cream and adding some caramel sauce, molasses, smashed peanuts, broken honeycomb (crush up a Crunchie Bar), etc., to take your ice cream sandwich into the stratosphere.

SHORTBREAD

THREE, TWO, ONE, THAT'S ALL IT IS.

200g salted butter, at room temperature

100g caster sugar

300g plain flour, sieved

Preheat the oven to 160°C and line a baking tray with greaseproof paper.

Make like Mary Berry and cream together the butter and sugar, with a wooden spoon (or with an electric whisk) until white. This will take some elbow grease, but with a recipe this simple, that is the least you can offer.

Add the flour a tablespoon at a time, beating to combine each time. Once it is all incorporated, bring the mix together with your hands. As per usual, do not overwork the dough. Like the cookie dough, place the shortbread mix on a sheet of greaseproof paper, roll it into a 7cm diameter sausage and roll it up and twist the ends like an old fashioned sweet. Chill in the fridge for 30 minutes.

When ready to cook, cut 1cm rounds out of your dough and place 2cm apart on a baking tray lined with greaseproof paper. Place in the oven and cook for 12–15 minutes until just golden on top. Remove from the oven and cool on a wire rack, sprinkling with a little extra caster sugar as they cool.

BROWNIES

240g cocoa powder

A pinch of salt

250g 70% dark chocolate

250g salted butter, at room temperature

500g caster sugar

6 medium eggs

240g plain flour

Preheat the oven to 180°C and grease and line a brownie tin with greaseproof paper.

Start by combining the flour, cocoa and salt in a large bowl, mix well and set aside.

Place the chocolate and butter in a heatproof bowl over a pan of gently simmering water until both have melted. Remove from the heat and stir to form a dark glossy mix. In a separate bowl, whisk together the eggs and sugar until airy and light in colour. Pour the chocolate mix into the eggs and sugar, stirring constantly. Add the flour mixture to the chocolate and stir until just combined – do not overmix it. People always over mix.

Pour this perfectly mixed mixture into the prepared brownie tin and bake in the hot oven for 35–40 minutes or until a crust forms on the top and the sides just begin to come away from the edges of the tin. Remove from the oven and leave the brownies in the tin to cool. Finally cut the perfect brownies into fist-sized squares and prepare to create a monster ice cream sandwich.

"IF YOU'RE FEELING SAD,
QUITE BAD NOT GLAD, OR MAD,
THEN WHY NOT MAKE A TREAT
YOU WANT TO EAT.

YOU'LL TURN THAT FROWNY,
RIGHT SIDE UP FROM UPSIDE DOWNY,
IF YOU COOK YOURSELF
A TRAY OF GOOEY BROWNIES"

BY SIEGFRIED TOOSOON, 1918

GINGER BISCUITS

YOU CAN QUITE CLEARLY BUY A BANGING MCVITIE'S GINGER NUT BISCUIT. AND IF THAT IS YOUR BAG, THEN DO SO. BUT THE FOLLOWING ARE DANGEROUSLY GOOD, AND MORE DOABLE THAN ONE MIGHT THINK, SO WHY NOT GIVE A BATCH A GO?

100g unsalted butter, plus extra for greasing

100g caster sugar

100g golden syrup

200g self-raising flour, plus extra for dusting

2 tsps ground ginger

Start by melting the butter, sugar and syrup together in a heavy-bottomed saucepan over a medium heat.

In a mixing bowl, combine the flour and ginger. Pour the melted butter et al into the bowl and mix to combine. As usual, do not overwork. Bring the dough together with your hands and roll into a cylinder. Wrap in greaseproof paper, twist the end like an old fashioned sweetie and chill in the fridge for 30 minutes.

Preheat the oven to 180°C. Line a baking tray with greaseproof paper.

Cut 1cm rounds from your chilled roll and lay them on a baking tray lined with greaseproof paper. Place in the hot oven to cook for 10 minutes. When ready, remove from the oven, allow to cool on the tray for 5 minutes and then cool fully on a wire rack.

BRIOCHE

BONJOUR. ÇA VA?

DONC VOUS AVEZ ESSAYÉ DES MACARONS? ET MAINTENANT VOUS PENSEZ QUE VOUS ÊTES UNE SORTE DE PAUL BERT? EH BIEN, BILLY GRANDE BOLLOCKS, PEUT-ÊTRE QUE L'HUMBLE BRIOCHE SERA VOTRE RUPTURE? BRAVO À VOUS POUR AVOIR ESSAYÉ, EN PARTICULIER FACE À UNE BRIOCHE COMMERCIALEMENT TRÈS BONNE. MAIS HONNÊTEMENT, NOUS VOUS APPLAUDISSONS, MÊME NOUS AURIONS PU METTRE NOS MAINS DANS NOS POCHES ET ACHETER LA BRIOCHE.

7g sachet of fast-action dried yeast

25ml warm water (ideally body temperature)

280g strong white bread flour

40g caster sugar

1 tsp salt

2 large eggs, plus 1 extra, for glazing

180g unsalted butter, room temperature and cut into cubes. Cut it when it's cold.

Combine the yeast and warm water and leave to sit and foam for about 15 minutes. Meanwhile, combine the flour, sugar and salt. When the yeast has bloomed (get us!), whisk the eggs vigorously into it before adding the whole thing to the flour mix and mix well with your hands to form a loose dough.

Transfer this dough to the bowl of an electric mixer on the slow setting and add the butter a few lumps at a time. Mix slowly so that the butter is well incorporated. When you have a nice wet dough, cover the bowl of the mixer with clingfilm and transfer to the fridge. It wants to chill out now for about 24 hours, although overnight is fine.

Turn out your dough onto a floured surface and, with lightly floured hands, shape the dough into a loaf shape that corresponds to the tin you are about to drop it into. Lift it into the tin and cover lightly with clingfilm. You want to leave this somewhere warm to rise for about 3 hours.

When you return to cook the brioche, preheat the oven to 200°C and line a loaf tin with baking parchment.

When the dough has risen (by about three times), brush the top of the loaf with some beaten egg, keeping the rest for later, and place in the hot oven. Immediately reduce the heat of the oven to 180°C and bake for 30 minutes. Remove the loaf from the oven and turn it out of its tin. Brush the whole loaf with the beaten egg and return to the oven, on a tray, for one last blast at 180°C for 10 minutes.

Remove the cooked loaf from the oven again and allow to cool on a wire rack.

CRUMPETS

130ml full fat milk

130ml warm water

7g sachet of fast-action dried yeast

110g plain flour

110g strong white flour

Salt

1 tsp caster sugar

½ tsp bicarbonate of soda

Start by warming the milk and water in a pan until just hotter than body temperature. Use your finger to tell. Add the yeast and leave to one side for 15 minutes to bloom and froth. Meanwhile, measure out your flours in a large bowl and add the salt. Slowly pour in the yeasty milk and water, whisking vigorously until you have a smooth batter. Cover with clingfilm and leave somewhere warm for 40 minutes to rise.

Once risen (it will bubble and rise only a little bit) add the bicarbonate of soda (and stir vigorously) before leaving to stand for another 20 minutes in a warm place.

Place a heavy-bottomed frying pan over a medium heat. Leave for a couple of minutes to get nice and hot before reducing the heat to its lowest flame.

When ready, oil the inside of a crumpet (pastry) ring, if you have one, and sit it in the pan. If you don't have a crumpet ring, don't worry, you can go freeform and people will love you all the more for it. Using a ladle, spoon some (1cm?) of the batter into the crumpet ring and allow to cook for 6–7 minutes until the top is almost cooked and full of holes.

Remove the ring and briefly flip the crumpet to gently brown the top and finish the cooking. After 30 seconds, remove the crumpet and scoff. Repeat for all those other crumpets you are about to devour.

MERINGUES

5 medium eggs, just whites

300g caster sugar

Preheat the oven to 100°C , and line a baking tray with greasproof paper, stuck down with a little oil underneath it.

Clean a mixing bowl and a whisk with sanitary precision. Show a similar dedication to the cleaning of your hands.

Crack the eggs into the bowl and pull out the yolks carefully with your hands. You should be left with pristine egg whites. Keep the yolks for an ice cream base or a custard or something, or throw them away.

Whisk the egg whites with an electric whisk, until you have achieved foamy soft peaks. Keep whisking while you add the sugar a little at a time. Whisk until you have perfectly firm and glossy peaks.

Spoon dollops of the meringue mix onto the lined baking tray, leaving plenty of room between each one, as they will spread as they cook.

Place in the hot oven for 40 minutes, then turn off the heat and leave the door slightly ajar. Leave them in the oven until the oven is completely cool. At this point you will have a perfect crispy meringue.

ICE CREAM

THIS RECIPE IS TWO THINGS; INCREDIBLY SIMPLE AND SIMPLY INCREDIBLE.

500ml full fat milk

500ml double cream

8 egg yolks

175g caster sugar

1 vanilla pod, split in half (optional)

If you have an ice cream machine, this is the recipe for you. If you don't, either buy one or skip ahead to the next recipe – it is the freezer aisle for you mon cherie.

In a mixing bowl, whisk the egg yolks and sugar with an electric whisk, until they are light and fluffy and white.

Heat the milk and cream (and vanilla, if you are using it) in a decent sized saucepan.

Once the milk and cream mixture has the occasional bubble blipping away on its surface, remove from the heat.

Add a little of the warm milk mixture to the egg yolks and mix well. Return all this mixture to the rest of the milk and cream in the pan and cook out until the custard coats the back of a wooden spoon and doesn't drip when you run your finger through it in a line on the back of the spoon. For those of you with a zest for precision, stop cooking the ice cream base once it has reached 80°C. Remove the vanilla pod (if using).

Allow your ice cream base to cool, before churning as it is in an ice cream machine (it is your machine so we presume you know how to use it, if not, find the manual) Most of the way through churning you can add any flavours, stewed fruit etc., you might fancy.

What follows is a list of recipes that are perfect on their own as well as being totally sensational when stirred through this ice cream base and then churned into a mind-bendingly good ice cream.

BERRY COMPOTE

If you happen to find yourself near a seasonally appropriate berry, this recipe is the best way to turn it from plump fruit to fresh compote. And it is fail-safe.

Weigh the fruit. Take the weight of fruit and add 20 per cent of that weight in caster sugar to the fruit. So if you had 100g of fruit, you are going to add 20g of sugar. Stir well to mix and then leave to sit for 10 minutes. Now you will have a perfect fresh compote. You can sieve this to remove any seeds. Or if you are a true naturist, leave as it is and devour as a drizzle across an ice cream sandwich, or churn it into an ice cream and be very pleased with yourself. If you are a maximalist, do both.

NEVER KNOWINGLY CAUSE
LOVE FULLY, SURPRISE T
FOR UNEXPE

RT, LIVE FOR THE MOMENT,
WORLD AND LISTEN OUT
ED MUSIC.

POACHED FRUITS

EVERY NOW AND AGAIN FOR SOME UNEXPECTED REASON YOU MIGHT FIND YOURSELF WITH AN ABUNDANCE OF FRUIT. BE IT APPLES, PEARS, PLUMS OR (UNLIKELY IN THIS COUNTRY) APRICOTS. IF THIS DOES HAPPEN, WE WANT YOU TO HAVE A TRUSTED RECIPE TO TURN TO.

400g fruit, peeled if apples/pears, cut in half and de-stoned if plums, apricots etc.

500ml water (this can be all or partially substituted for wine if the fancy takes you)

125g caster sugar

2 cloves

1 cinnamon stick

1 vanilla pod, split in half

1 peeling of lemon zest

Juice of ¼ lemon

Find a heavy-bottomed and lidded saucepan and place over a medium heat. Add the water, sugar, cloves, cinnamon, vanilla pod and lemon zest to the pan and bring to the boil to dissolve the sugar.

Add the fruit to the pan and bring back to the boil. Turn the heat down to the lowest simmer and cover with the lid. Cook for 40 minutes. Check the fruit at this juncture, with the tip of a knife, and judge its cookedness. Soft flesh is good to go, firm flesh needs a little more time. Cook a little longer if needs be, or remove and cool if they are ready.

You can use the fruit in many ways. You will also have some killer syrup. We would recommend straining this off and reducing it until it's nice and thick. This can then be drizzled over things, whipped into things or used in an ice cream or maybe a cocktail.

CHOCOLATE SAUCE

THIS IS THE BEST CHOCOLATE SAUCE IN THE WHOLE WORLD. IT BREAKS ALL THE RULES OF CHOCOLATE COOKERY, AND THAT MAKES IT A FUCKING BADASS.

225g 70% dark chocolate, smashed up a bit

80g caster sugar

120ml double cream

60ml boiling water

Trust us with this recipe. Place all the ingredients in a saucepan and place over a medium heat. Slowly melt everything together without stirring. Once the chocolate appears completely melted, stir a few times and take off the heat.

This works perfectly as a chocolate sauce. If you are of the inclination, it also works perfectly stirred into a plain ice cream base to create a badass chocolate ice cream. Your call. It can be stored in an airtight container or jar in the fridge for millennia.

SALTED CARAMEL

100ml water

240g caster sugar

½ tsp salt

200ml double cream

You don't have to but it is a good idea to have a sugar thermometer for this kind of thing.

REMEMBER THERE IS NOTHING ON EARTH WORSE THAN BEING BURNED BY MOLTEN SUGAR.

Combine the water, sugar and salt in a heavy-bottomed saucepan and place over a medium heat. Do not stir. Simply swill the pan to let the sugar dissolve and start to bubble and darken. After roughly 5–6 minutes, you should have a nice chestnut-coloured caramel. Reduce the heat to its lowest flame and add the cream. It will spit and fizz, but do not be alarmed – continue to swill the pan in circular motions and soon enough you will have a homogenous caramel sauce. At this point, you can introduce a wooden spoon for the first time. Continue to cook out the sauce while you stir it for another 3 minutes or until it reads 200°C on your thermometer.

Transfer the sauce to a heatproof container and leave on the side to cool. It will thicken as it cools.

You can now spread it fully across the plains of your body, or, cover things with it, eat it, add it to milkshakes, churn it into ice creams, pour it all over ice cream inside one of your cut in half brownies, anything you like. Use your imagination – you can journey far and wide with this sauce. It gets on particularly well with Ottolenghi's favourite, pomegranate molasses.

BUTTERSCOTCH

"WHAT'S THE DIFFERENCE?" I HEAR YOU CRY. CARAMEL-SHARAMEL, BUTTERSCOTCH-SMUTTERSCOTCH. BUTTER IS THE DIFFERENCE! MY FRIEND JAMES BRIDLE'S GRANNY ONCE TOLD HIM THAT "THE DIFFERENCE BETWEEN A GOOD COOK AND A GREAT COOK, IS HALF A POUND OF BUTTER." BALLER.

100g unsalted butter, cubed

240g dark brown sugar

200ml double cream

½ tsp salt

REMEMBER THERE IS NOTHING ON EARTH WORSE THAN BEING BURNED BY MOLTEN SUGAR.

Add the butter to a heavy-bottomed saucepan and melt over a high heat until it is frothing gently. Add the sugar in one go and stir well. It will go a little thick and sandy, but keep cooking, keep stirring, and keep watching. After 3 or so minutes it will start to become smooth and loose. That is your cue to add the cream. Bang it all in at once and stir like a nutjob. It will spit and bubble a little, but keep stirring.

You can reduce the heat to low now and leave it blipping away, stirring every three minutes or so. After 10 minutes, you will have a perfectly smooth butterscotch sauce. Add the salt, leave it to stand for another couple of minutes and then give it a taste. Good, right?

HONEYCOMB

THIS SHIT WILL SEND YOU SNOOKER LOOPY. HOW GOOD IS A CRUNCHIE BAR? WELL, NOW YOU CAN MAKE YOUR OWN. MAKE A BATCH OF THIS, BREAK IT INTO CHUNKS AND DIP THEM IN MELTED CHOCOLATE, BREAK SOME AND EAT LIKE THAT AS A SNACK. CRUSH IT AND SCATTER OVER YOGHURT OR ICE CREAM, WHY WOULDN'T YOU?

375g caster sugar

125ml water

225g golden syrup

15g bicarbonate of soda

REMEMBER THERE IS NOTHING ON EARTH WORSE THAN BEING BURNED BY MOLTEN SUGAR.

Before you start, line a high-sided baking tray with greaseproof paper, stuck down with tiny bit of oil and leave to one side.

Place the sugar, water and syrup in a heavy-bottomed saucepan over a high heat. Do not stir it, but swill it around to dissolve and then watch as it darkens and becomes a caramel. Once it is the colour of dark wood, remove from the heat and add the bicarbonate of soda. It will froth and spit terrifyingly at this point. Keep calm and gently whisk the caramel as it turns into honeycomb.

Turn the resulting liquid out into your lined baking tray and leave it to cool and set. Do not touch it or mess about with it, this will knock air out of it and it will burn you worse than you could have imagined. You want a light, crispy honeycomb, and that comes from leaving it well alone.

Once it has cooled and set, you can do with it what you will. Turn it out and smash it into pieces, cut it into bites, or blitz it to dust and churn it through an ice cream or mix into yoghurt or something.

NUT BRITTLES

THIS IS GENUINELY ONE OF THE EASIEST THINGS IN THE WORLD, AND PEOPLE WILL THINK YOU ARE A PROPER GENIUS WHEN YOU SERVE IT TO THEM ON OR IN THEIR DESSERT.

300g salted peanuts

500g caster sugar

¼ tsp salt

REMEMBER THERE IS NOTHING ON EARTH WORSE THAN BEING BURNED BY MOLTEN SUGAR.

Start by lining a baking tray with baking parchment.

We've covered caramel, right? Well the first bit is just making another caramel. Sugar in pan, medium heat, swill don't stir and watch for a light mahogany colour. Done.

When you have reached peak caramel, add your nuts, give the whole thing a stir, and turn out onto your lined baking tray. Level with the back of a spoon and then leave to cool. How brilliant was that? Now cut it, break it, smash it or blitz it.

MOLASSES

This isn't a recipe, but more a note to say molasses are awesome. We're not talking here about the bootstrap treacle sort of molasses, although their sherbetty sweetness does of course have a time and a place. We are talking about fruit molasses. Pomegranate, tamarind, damson, etc. These are the reduced, thickened juices of fruit, and they are sweet and sour dynamite.

Pour some over ice cream, churn some into ice cream, drink it from the bottle for all we care. The point is, buy molasses, use it on your desserts, use it in salad dressings, we use the pomegranate version, on all our Spuds side dishes at The Sandwich Shop. And often use the tamarind one on our puddings. It is similar to pomegranate but darker and more bitter, which helps temper the sweetness of things.

SOREEN MALT LOAF CRISPS

Again, not a recipe really. Buy a loaf of Soreen. Put it in the freezer. Once frozen cut it into the thinnest slices you can manage with a serrated knife and lay these on a piece of greasproof paper on a baking tray. Try and do it unfrozen and you'll see why you freeze it. Heat an oven to 100°C and place the tray in the oven. Leave for 2 hours. Voilà! Malt Loaf Crisps! Like the nut brittle (p.285), you can keep these in whole slices to have with ice cream or break it and smash it and sprinkle it over or even into your ice cream as it churns.

This works just as well with Jamaica Ginger Cake.

MALT POWDER AND ITS INFINITE USES

Have you ever met anyone who doesn't like Maltesers?

Buy a bag/jar of malt powder, Horlicks or a cheaper one, and start sprinkling it on and in every sweet dish you make. That deep-ovaltine-umami-sweetness is a donkey-kick for your taste buds, and sometimes they need that. So give 'em what they want.

VANILLA CREAM

THIS IS LIKE PANNACOTTA BUT LOOSER. WE USE IT AT THE SANDWICH SHOP TO GO OVER CHOUX PASTRY BUNS FILLED WITH BALLS OF ICE CREAM. NAUGHTY. WE'VE BEEN KNOWN TO PUT NUT BRITTLE ON TOP OF THAT TOO.

250ml double cream

30g icing sugar

½ tsp vanilla extract

1 sheet gelatin, soaked in cold water for at least 10 minutes

Add the cream, sugar and vanilla extract to a small pan and warm over a low flame. When a dipped finger can detect a little heat, remove from the heat and thoroughly whisk in the soaked gelatin.

Divide into portions or a single low bowl. Place in the fridge and allow to set for 2 hours at least.

NUT BUTTERS

500g skinless nuts – preferably a singular nut, be it almond (works best), or hazelnut (works almost as well) or peanut (works just as well), etc.

Rapeseed oil

Salt

Preheat the oven to 170°C

Lay out your nuts on a greaseproof paper lined roasting tray. Place in the hot oven and roast for 6–8 minutes or until coloured nicely and not looking too brown.

While still warm, place in a food processor and blitz continuously for a good 5 minutes. The nuts will start to form a buttery mess, so you may have to scrape down the sides a few times. Add some oil (the exact amount depends on the nuts, the speed of your blender, the texture you are after, but start with 1 tablespoon) and whizz whilst the nuts get buttery-er and smoother. Add a little more oil if you want to go smoother or just add the salt if you are happy. When happy, transfer to a jar or container and keep for those moments when you just want to eat spoonful after spoonful in your pants. You can use in other ways too, but that'll likely be your second batch. This batch is for smug little you, in your pants.

BISCUIT SPREADS

Been given an excess of shortbread for Christmas? Got a surfeit of digestives? Put them in a food processor and blitz blitz blitz. Leave the motor running for a full 2 minutes — it will warm the mix and encourage the fat to break out and create a smooth, paste. If you like, add some honey or maple syrup for sweetness, viscosity and shine. Some incredibly naughty people have been known to drizzle melted butter in while they are blending (like a cheesecake base). If you'd like something really smooth you will have to add a drizzle of vegetable oil. We like rapeseed.

Woody Creek, CO

Dear Mr. Burgess,

Herr Wenner has forwarded your useless letter from Rome to the National Affairs Desk for my examination and/or reply.

Unfortunately, we have no International Gibberish Desk, or it would have ended up there.

What kind of lame, half-mad bullshit are you trying to sneak over on us? When Rolling Stone asks for "a thinkpiece," goddamnit, we want a fucking Thinkpiece ... and don't try to weasel out with any of your limey bullshit about a "50,000 word novella about the condition humaine, etc..."

Do you take us for a gang of brainless lizards? Rich hoodlums? Dilettante thugs?

You lazy cocksucker. I want that Thinkpiece on my desk by Labor Day. And I want it ready for press. The time has come & gone when cheapjack scum like you can get away with the kind of scams you got rich from in the past.

Get your worthless ass out of the piazza and back to the typewriter. Your type is a dime a dozen around here, Burgess, and I'm fucked if I'm going to stand for it any longer.

Sincerely,

Hunter S. Thompson

Third

First

Second

INDEX

Page numbers in **bold** refer to Max's Sandwiches. Page numbers in *italics* refer to photographs.